*A new global Faith that*

- Offers spiritual transformation and fulfillment
- Unifies the world under one God and one Faith
- Restores religion's lost purpose and purity
- Unveils life's meaning and purpose
- Provides a haven of hope and peace in today's troubled world

### What if You Found a Faith that Answered all Your Questions?

...the highest and purest form of religious teaching...I know of no other [faith] so profound.     Leo Tolstoy

...deserves the best thought we can give it.     Helen Keller

# Bahá'í Faith

## *God's Greatest Gift to Humankind*

Second Edition

Hushidar Hugh Motlagh, Ed.D.

www.globalperspective.org

**Website:** www.globalperspective.org

**Email:** info@globalperspective.org

Address:  Global Perspective
1106 Greenbanks Dr.
Mt. Pleasant, MI 48858
USA

**Phone:** 989-772-1432

**Fax:** 989-772-1432

Cover design by Lori Block

Cover photo by Marco Abrar—www.BahaiPictures.com

ISBN: 0937661333
LCCN: 2006924978

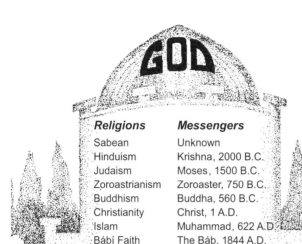

| Religions | Messengers |
|---|---|
| Sabean | Unknown |
| Hinduism | Krishna, 2000 B.C. |
| Judaism | Moses, 1500 B.C. |
| Zoroastrianism | Zoroaster, 750 B.C. |
| Buddhism | Buddha, 560 B.C. |
| Christianity | Christ, 1 A.D. |
| Islam | Muhammad, 622 A.D. |
| Bábí Faith | The Báb, 1844 A.D. |
| Bahá'í Faith | Bahá'u'lláh, 1863 A.D. |

*I shall come again and receive you to myself.* Christ

*I am the Alpha and the Omega, the First and the Last, the Beginning and the End.* Christ

*Whenever there is decay of righteousness...then I Myself come forth...for the sake of firmly establishing righteousness. I am born from age to age.* Krishna

*I am not the first Buddha who came upon the earth, nor shall I be the last. In due time another Buddha will arise... He shall reveal to you the same eternal truths which I have taught you.* Buddha

*All these holy, divine Manifestations are one. They have served one God, promulgated the same truth...and reflected the same light...In name and form they differ, but in reality They agree and are the same.* Bahá'u'lláh

*The Revelation of God may be likened to the sun. No matter how innumerable its risings, there is but one sun, and upon it depends the life of all things.* The Báb

# Books in This Series

## Others

# A Seven-Piece Puzzle

This book is the first part of a seven-volume series that are complementary to each other even as pieces of a single puzzle. To see the beautiful picture of human life and destiny—what God has planned for each of us here and hereafter—it is essential to study *all seven volumes, preferably in the following order*:

| | |
|---|---|
| 1. *Bahá'í Faith: God's Greatest Gift to Humankind*, 160 pages. | This volume describes briefly the teachings and history of the Bahá'í Faith. *It displays the fruits of the Tree of Life*. |
| 2. *Bahá'u'lláh: The One Promised in All Scriptures*, 235 pages.  | This volume describes the life and Mission of the One who established the Bahá'í Faith. *This is the root of the Tree of life, and the most significant volume in this series*. Reading it is a must for every seeker of truth. |

| | |
|---|---|
| 3. *Proofs of the Bahá'í Faith.*<br> | The One who has sent Messengers to us has also given us clear and definitive standards by which they can be recognized. This book applies those standards to Bahá'u'lláh and proves that He has fulfilled every one of them on a scale never seen before. |
| 4. *The Greatest News: The News Everyone Should Hear,* 166 pages.<br> | This book is addressed primarily to Christians. It proves that *Bahá'u'lláh—the Glory of God—fulfills the promise of the second coming of Christ.* |
| 5. *Death: The Door to Heaven,* 182 pages.<br> | This volume describes the mysteries of the afterlife as revealed by Bahá'u'lláh. *It explains the meaning of hell and heaven and shows how we can attain our divine destiny, how we can prepare our soul for God's "many Mansions in heaven"* (John 14:2). Without gaining a glimpse of the afterlife, this life has no meaning. |

# A Seven-Piece Puzzle

| | |
|---|---|
| 6. *God's 19 Great Little Tranquilizers*, 62 pages.<br><br> | We have been created to know and love God. This small book presents the "*Knowledge of God*." It sets forth what we need to know about our Creator to attain a state of utter joy and peace. It reveals the spiritual design of creation and presents 19 principles that lead us to a life of contentment and happiness. |
| 7. *Bahá'í Prayers*, 230 pages.<br><br> | We are asked to recognize a tree by its fruits (Matthew 7:20). Prayers are the first fruits of religion—its heart and soul. They are the heavenly lights that guide us to the presence of God and manifest His glory and grandeur. The prayers offered in this book are a basketful of fruits from the Vineyard of *Bahá'u'lláh—the Glory of God*. |

The prime purpose of this series is to unveil our *glorious destiny* and to demonstrate how the teachings of Bahá'u'lláh can help us:

❋ *To know God more truly*

❋ *To love Him more intimately*

* *To trust Him more genuinely, and*

 * *To submit to His Will and His Wisdom more willingly.*

Reading the preceding volumes in the recommended order will lead you toward the discovery of the greatest mysteries of human life and destiny. It will help you resolve these puzzling and profound questions: *Who are we? Why are we here? Where are we going? And how can we fulfill our divine destiny—attain the very purpose for which we have come into this world?* Are there, and will there ever be, any concerns and questions that are more urgent and of a greater consequence?

# The Promise of All Ages

The desired of all nations shall come.
Haggai 2:7

He who is the Desired One is come in His transcendent majesty...Better is this for you than all ye possess.[1]
Bahá'í Scriptures

And I...am about to come and gather all nations and tongues, and they will come and see my glory.    Isaiah 66:18

All nations and kindreds...will become a single nation. Religious and sectarian antagonism, the hostility of races and peoples, and differences among nations, will be eliminated.[2]
Bahá'í Scriptures

The old order of things has passed away...I am making everything new.
Revelation 21:4-5 NIV

Soon will the present-day order be rolled up, and a new one spread out in its stead.[3]    Bahá'í Scriptures

## *The Light of Unity*

Ye are the fruits of one tree, and the leaves of one branch. Deal ye one with another with the utmost love and harmony, with friendliness and fellowship ...So powerful is the light of unity that it can illuminate the whole earth. The One true God, He Who knoweth all things, Himself testifieth to the truth of these words.[4]    Bahá'í Scriptures

# Why a New Religion?

The time has come to bring people together. There is a religion that can do this. It is the most powerful unifying force in the world today. It has gathered under its wings millions from every race, creed, and culture. Only once in a thousand years does a revelation of such stature dawn upon the planet. It is the religion promised in all the Holy Scriptures, the faith to unite all faiths, the light of hope and peace mankind has been waiting for since the dawn of history. It seems too good, but it is true. It is called "the Bahá'í Faith," and its followers, "the Bahá'ís," namely "those who follow the Light."

This book offers you the basic facts of the new Faith, and an opportunity to see for yourself the astonishing benefits it has in store for you and for the world.

> You hold…the key that will settle all of our difficulties…
>
> Dr. George Washington Carver

# Contents

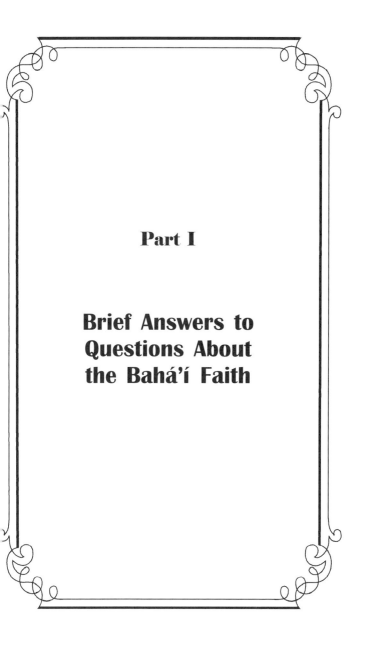

# Part I

# Brief Answers to Questions About the Bahá'í Faith

# One God, One Faith
# One People

## *The most challenging and rewarding search*

Within the last two centuries our way of life has been altered by a massive scientific and technological revolution. To balance this, we desperately need a spiritual revolution of the same magnitude. Many are unaware that in the mid-19th century a religion was born with the clear goal of achieving this objective, namely revolutionizing the spiritual life of the world. The following are very brief responses to some of the questions people ask frequently about this religion: the Bahá'í Faith.

## *What is the Bahá'í Faith?*

It is a world religion born in 1844. Its followers are called *Bahá'ís,* meaning "those who follow the light." Its prime goal is to spiritualize humanity, to make religion relevant to our time, to restore its purity and vitality, and to focus and direct its energies toward the goal of creating a world society based on justice, peace, and unity.

The Bahá'í teachings remove the obstacles that prevent people from manifesting their highest potential. They cultivate positive and critical thinking, self-esteem, self-actualization, and enlightened faith. Dogmatism has no place in the Bahá'í Faith.

By fostering the knowledge of God and the love of God, the Bahá'í Faith opens a new dimension to life's inner harmony and peace. In the light of its teachings, life glows with an enduring purpose, it changes from a depressive and monotonous cycle into an everlasting adventure of hope and fulfillment. Without a cosmic and eternal perspective, which can come only from knowing and loving God, life loses its luster, its enduring purpose and excitement.

## *Who are the central figures of the Bahá'í Faith?*

Its central figures are the ***Báb,*** meaning "***the Gate,***" ***Bahá'u'lláh,*** meaning "***the Glory of God,***" and ***'Abdu'l-Bahá,*** meaning "***the Servant of Glory.***" The Báb was the Herald of Bahá'u'lláh and came to prepare the way for Him. The Báb, condemned for His claim, was executed in 1850. Bahá'u'lláh, the founder of the Bahá'í Faith, brought a vast store of knowledge and left Scriptures equal to a hundred volumes. 'Abdu'l-Bahá, Bahá'u'lláh's son, served as an example to inspire the hearts and translate the Bahá'í teachings into a life of active service to humanity.

## *Do Bahá'ís believe in God?*

Yes, they do! They refer to God as "the unknowable Essence" who stands transcendent above human comprehension. No being can ever fully know the Creator's identity or essence. The best anyone can do is to recognize some of His names and attributes.

To help us and make us aware of Himself, God selects Messengers (also called Mediators, Redeemers, and Teachers) and grants them special distinctions and honors. Through them He provides us spiritual guidance. His Messengers, because of the great favors bestowed on them, become His most intimate and devoted "friends." Since they recognize His infinite perfections, they glorify and adore His wonders beyond measure. They follow His bidding, and stand firm in their love and devotion for Him.

Their main goal is to teach us so that we also may learn to ***know***, ***love***, and ***glorify*** God—the One who gave us the gift of life. This knowledge, love, and devotion are the most powerful motivators in all the universe. They can uplift an individual from the depths of immorality, selfishness, despondency, and gloom to the highest and richest realms of purity, peace, hope, and happiness.

No joy can compare with the joy of knowing, loving, serving, and glorifying God. The purpose of religion is to spread and strengthen this love, knowledge, and devotion and to bring them into every heart and every home. Without God our world turns into a place of gloom and darkness, and our hearts into abodes of emptiness.

When a religion loses its transforming powers, it becomes an instrument of division and discord rather than unity and harmony. It promotes rote learning rather than reasoning. Consequently, people begin to lose their faith and their sense of "connectedness" with other human beings. They wonder why God does not care any more. They blame Him for their troubles and sufferings, and eventually ignore His counsels. When people lose touch with God, they also lose touch with themselves. Knowledge of God leads to knowledge of self; ignorance of God leads to ignorance of self.

Bahá'u'lláh can once again restore God's love to the heart of humanity by making religion rational and relevant to our time. Bahá'ís believe that Bahá'u'lláh's Revelation is a clear proof that God *cares* and *will always care.* In the teachings of the Bahá'í Faith, we can find peace, hope, and harmony. By the guidance it provides, we can resolve the world's distressing problems. Through Bahá'u'lláh's teachings we can build a heavenly kingdom, a glorious civilization that has been the promise of all the great Messengers, and the hope of humanity since the dawn of history.

## *Why do we need a new religion?*

Most of the problems we face in the world are caused by low moral standards. Historically, when these standards descend to a critical point, God sends a new Teacher or Messenger to help us become more just, loving and kind. We have already passed that low point.

What is the source of moral values? Religion. How can moral values be strengthened? By making religion rational and relevant. This is exactly what the Bahá'í Faith has done.

Bahá'ís believe that what we need today, more than anything else, are these:

- A sense of dignity and nobility.

- A cosmic and global perspective; a feeling of being connected to the whole universe and all humanity.

- An undying and eternal purpose.

- A rational understanding of religion.

- A new commitment to ethical values.

- A new vision about who we are, what we are doing, and where we are going. Without this new vision and new perspective we will operate on a level of narrow self-interest and confusion. Hedonism becomes our goal and god.

## *How can I know the Bahá'í Faith is true?*

In recognizing or testing the truth of a religion, we should begin with two questions:

- Why have the masses of people always rejected God's Messengers?

- What makes *my* religion true?

By clarifying or resolving these two questions, *we open new doors that will lead us to an objective knowledge of truth*. When we realize that most of those who met Noah, Abraham, Moses, or Jesus, failed to recognize their greatness, we learn to be more humble. A mountain climber who knows many others have tried and failed to conquer the crest of a mountain, will not be complacent about his victory. He will examine every evidence, he will follow every lead, he will investigate every clue that might tell him why other climbers did not succeed, and how he might overcome their obstacles.

Similarly, when we examine the reasons why we believe in our own religion and what makes our religion true for us, we learn to become more objective in judging our beliefs.

First, let us list some causes that have always led people to reject God's Messengers and Redeemers:

- Not understanding the symbolism behind prophecies.

- Expecting earth shaking or miraculous events.

- Being apathetic, having no interest in religion.

- Following the majority, assuming that they are the best judge.

- Depending on religious leaders who regard tradition as the truth.

- Being too busy; not finding time to devote to spiritual matters.

- Being worldly and selfish. Not looking beyond self-interest.

- Not wishing to alienate friends or family members.

- Fearing false prophets.

Most or perhaps all of these reasons can be summarized in these words: ***unawareness*** and ***closedmindedness***. Those to whom God's Messengers and Redeemers were sent, either did not look, or if they ***did*** look, they saw only what they wanted to see. To be open-minded, a person must follow two steps:

- Make a thorough search to find the facts.

- Judge the facts objectively.

Let us now consider the other question, namely what makes ***my*** religion true? When confronted with this question, many Christians think of the birth and resurrection of Jesus. They believe these were His ultimate proofs. More liberal Christians think of Jesus Himself: His words and deeds. Of course, many base their faith on both, namely Jesus as a person and His miracles. Those who consider miracles the prime proof become disappointed when they learn that many "pagans" also base the proof of their beliefs on miracles. Because the "pagans" present glowing testimonials about their gods; they attribute to them the most astonishing wonders. How can we tell who is right or who is wrong? We face an impossible task. Miracles are definitely un-reliable, especially for those who have not wit-nessed them.

Those who regard Jesus Himself as the essential evidence can never be disappointed. For His thoughts, His words, and His deeds are clearly distinct and distinguished. An ordinary person can in no way compete with His excellence.

The Gospel is a remarkable evidence of a supreme Spirit at work. It portrays the life of a humble and heavenly figure endowed with supreme courage, di-vine wisdom, flawless character, and a far-reaching vision. It shows the sudden dawning of a new light in the darkness of discord and desolation. Should we not test Bahá'u'lláh by the same standards? The remarkable story of the advent of Bahá'u'lláh and His Herald the Báb is offered in great detail later in this book. (See Part II.)

## *How do Bahá'ís intend to unite the diverse religions of the world?*

A famous poet tells a story about three travelers who spoke different languages. During their journey they found a coin. And since they could not divide it, they decided to buy some food and then divide the food. Their inability to communicate led to a heated argument. At that point a fourth person who spoke all three languages came to their aid. And when he listened to their argument, he smiled and said: "You all want the same fruit, namely grapes."

People worship the same God, and ask Him for the same favors and blessings. They want happiness, contentment, security, comfort, and peace. But in spite of their common goals, they stand divided.

Through their belief in "the progressive revelation of truth" Bahá'ís can communicate with the followers of all great religions. Within the past century and a half they have unified millions of people from every religion, race, creed, and culture. The new faith is a laboratory in which the unity of religion has been tested and tried with phenomenal success.

People have been taught to believe that their religion is the only true religion—the only way to the Kingdom of Heaven—and they tend to accept this as an unquestionable fact. As long as they have not examined other religions with an open mind, they can persist with their beliefs. But what happens when they take one step beyond the boundaries of tradition? They begin to notice an astonishing similarity between the fundamental teachings of all the great religions of the world. Once they see this, they find it hard to go back to their original beliefs. Like a person who is told his hometown is the best, he can believe it as long as he has not ventured into other towns.

Bahá'u'lláh creates a new awareness and a new understanding of religion. Once people gain this awareness and insight, they exclaim: "It is so refreshing to learn about a faith that respects all faiths."

Even though people believe in the uniqueness of their religion, somehow they sense that this belief does not fit in with their understanding of a benevolent Creator who loves all His children. They hear a Voice in their soul murmuring: "The Creator cannot descend to a level lower than humans. He cannot care for some of His children, and ignore or abandon the rest."

In my youth I had read various passages from the Qur'án from time to time. At one point I decided to read it from cover to cover. During this reading I was overtaken by a sense of awe and mystery. The feeling came from hearing the same Voice I had heard many a time before, during repeated readings of the Bible. I can never forget that unearthly experience.

## *What is the Bahá'í plan for world peace?*

"Though the mountains be shaken and the hills be removed, yet my unfailing love for you will not be shaken nor my covenant of peace be removed," says the Lord, who has compassion on you.                                    Isaiah 54:10 NIV

Bahá'u'lláh teaches that world peace can come only through world unity. If the various nations, religions, and races were united, there would be no reason for war. But without unity, war or preparation for war will continue.

Had humanity responded promptly to Bahá'u'lláh's plan for peace, World War I and World War II would not have happened. Similarly, if the world awakens to the relevance and urgency of the Bahá'í teachings now, the forces that generate war will disappear. War is a symptom of a disease. The disease is disunity. As soon as Bahá'u'lláh's uniting remedy is applied, the disease will vanish.

We all have a responsibility to do our share to free the human race from the scourge of war. We should not underestimate our capacity to change the world. What brings about the change, what generates love and peace and unity is always God's Power. We need to empty ourselves and, like a reed, allow God's Voice to awaken and enchant us, and to echo that Voice until it is heard in every part of the world by every citizen of our planet.

## *Why do Bahá'ís emphasize "independent search for truth"?*

To study the principle of independent investigation, we need to do some soul-searching. And a good way to do the soul-searching is to begin with this question: what would be my religion, if I were raised in:

- a Hindu family?
- a Jewish family?
- a Buddhist family?
- a Muslim family?
- an agnostic family?
- an atheist family?

Most people admit that their religion would consist of whatever their parents taught them. What does this suggest? That most people are satisfied with and regard as truth what their ancestors believed and practiced. One's religion is thus determined by chance and is often accepted without investigation.

> The secret of happiness is freedom and the secret of freedom is courage.

> Give me the liberty to know, to think, to believe, and to utter freely, according to conscience, above all liberties.

Bahá'u'lláh declares that religion is too important to be left to chance and imitation, that every individual should examine other religions and other ways of life, and then choose his own direction. No loss can come from seeking, from gaining knowledge and awareness. In fact, just the opposite happens. Every good comes from seeking, and every evil from not seeking—from closing the mind.

> True opinions can prevail only if the facts to which they refer are known; if they are not known, false ideas are just as effective as true ones, if not a little more effective.

By far the most important freedom is spiritual freedom. For every consequence is temporary except the spiritual. As the noted author, Dr. Wayne Dyer, states:

> Learning to be detached from the past and the traditions that are an important part of many people's lives is one way to eliminate some of the suffering that exists in our world. Take a look at all of the people who are fighting in wars around the globe today, and you see them suffering and

dying in the name of tradition. They are taught that what their ancestors believed is what they must believe. With this logic they perpetuate the suffering in their own lives and in the lives of their assigned enemies.[1]

We can respect and even appreciate the past and the ways of our ancestors. We can love them for having chosen to go their own way. But to be attached to having to live and think the way others before you did, because you showed up looking like them in form, is to deny yourself enlightenment. This is how people and their institutions have controlled others for thousands of years.[2]

There is a time when we must firmly choose the spiritual course that we will follow, or the relentless drift of events will make the decision for us.

### *How does an open-minded person find the truth?*

- He has a deep desire to find it and pursues it with unwavering resolve. He searches for truth as urgently as a person who has lost a jewel.

- He tests everything *for himself* and does not depend on others—parents or pastors—to judge or decide for him. He refuses to seek safety in tradition or popularity.

- Selfish interests do not stand in his way: "How will my friends react?" "What will my parents say?" Such questions may enter his mind, but they do not affect his judgment.

- He erases from his mind all preconceived notions. Like a member of a jury, he begins with a clear slate. (Some people even allow a new name to affect their judgment. They refuse to study the Bahá'í Faith because, they say, it "sounds" strange!)

- He is sincere; he does not argue merely to win a point.

- He is patient and persistent, and willingly invests time and effort.

- He trusts God and constantly prays for His help.

If an individual lacks, or fails to acquire, any of these seven qualities, he is spiritually handicapped. Discovering and overcoming one's special handicaps is the first step in the path of the search for truth. Taking this first step is perhaps the most challenging task.

The fact that all the divine Messengers have been rejected by the masses of humanity is the best evidence of how difficult and vital it is to practice "independent search for truth," and why this principle is so unique, so consequential.

If you are open-minded, you will attain the greatest good. For the mind is the first gate to wisdom, truth, and happiness. After the mind has done its work, the heart must prepare a place and welcome the truth with warmth, joy, and gratitude.

# *What other teachings did Bahá'u'lláh bring for fostering a prosperous and harmonious world?*

These are a few:

- *Universal and compulsory education.* Education should cultivate not only the mind but the character as well. In fact, the latter is more vital than the former.

- *Equality of men and women.* Each gender has special talents and can make special contributions to society. Women have had fewer opportunities for developing their talents. Their role or influence in raising children makes them especially deserving of new and greater opportunities for self-enhancement.

- *Elimination of poverty.* There should be a fair distribution of wealth. The Bahá'í Faith has laws and teachings that make this possible.

- *Work is not a curse or a burden, but a blessing and a gift from God.* In the estimation of God, Bahá'u'lláh teaches, work is as noble as worship. All are encouraged to invest their talents in a craft or profession.

- *Elimination of prejudice.* Being prejudiced is identical with being closed-minded. A mind that is already set in a special way stands as an obstacle to understanding, harmony, peace, and unity.

- *A new world order*. A religion that intends to unite the world, must set an example of order and unity in the way it directs its own affairs. The Bahá'í Faith offers such a model of unity.

- *Universal auxiliary language*. As the world shrinks, communication between its inhabitants becomes more critical. A universal auxiliary language is an essential medium for fostering fellowship and understanding among nations.

## *How do Bahá'ís reconcile religion and science?*

Science reveals the truths and mysteries of the physical world; religion those of the spiritual. Each concerns itself with a separate but interdependent dimension of the universe. Seldom do the sacred Scriptures address scientific issues. There are a few exceptions, for instance, a Qur'anic verse declares that the sun is a flowing and stationary body (Qur'án 36:37-38; see also *Some Answered Questions,* Chapter 7). This knowledge contradicted the prevailing view of the time. Scientists also avoid involvement in religious issues.

Why then does conflict emerge? It emerges mostly from literal-mindedness. Aside from their message, the sacred Scriptures are masterpieces of literature. They contain an abundance of figures of speech. Understanding the symbolism behind metaphoric verses requires imagination and openness. The dogmatic believers, who often present themselves as the only model of true faith and understanding, are as a rule quite literal minded.

This ***seemingly*** harmless and trivial handicap leads to devastating consequences:

- It causes a rift between religion and science and thereby destroys religion's dignity in the eyes of the enlightened believers and seekers of truth.

- It prevents people from understanding the symbolic meaning of prophecies, which in turn leads to the denial of divine Messengers.

## *Do Bahá'ís pray?*

Yes, Bahá'ís have a spiritual obligation to pray every day. This is an example of a daily prayer:

> I bear witness, O my God, that Thou hast created me to know Thee and to worship Thee. I testify, at this moment, to my powerlessness and to Thy might, to my poverty and to Thy wealth.
>
> There is none other God but Thee, the Help in Peril, the Self-Subsisting.[3]

A prayer for those in difficulties:

> Is there any Remover of difficulties save God? Say: Praised be God! He is God! All are His servants and all abide by His bidding![4]

A morning prayer:

> I have wakened in Thy shelter, O my God, and it becometh him that seeketh that shelter to abide

within the Sanctuary of Thy protection and the Stronghold of Thy defense. Illumine my inner being, O my Lord, with the splendors of the Day-Spring of Thy Revelation, even as Thou didst illumine my outer being with the morning light of Thy favor.[5]

## *Do Bahá'ís have their own Scriptures?*

Bahá'u'lláh wrote Scriptures equal to a hundred volumes. The Báb and 'Abdu'l-Bahá also wrote extensively. Bahá'ís believe that the Word of God contains creative powers that illuminate and transform the hearts of humanity. The following key quotations from Bahá'í Scriptures are inscribed over the alcoves and entrances to the Bahá'í House of Worship in Wilmette, Illinois:

All the prophets of God proclaim the same faith.

Religion is a radiant light and an impregnable stronghold.

Ye are the fruits of one tree, and the leaves of one branch.

So powerful is unity's light that it can illumine the whole earth.

Consort with the followers of all religions with friendliness.

O Son of Being! Thou art My lamp and My light is in thee.

O Son of Being! Walk in My statutes for love of Me.

Thy Paradise is My love; thy heavenly home reunion with Me.

The light of a good character surpasseth the light of the sun.[6]

The earth is but one country, and mankind its citizens.

The best beloved of all things in My sight is justice; turn not away therefrom if thou desirest Me.

My love is My stronghold; he that entereth therein is safe and secure.

Breathe not the sins of others so long as thou art thyself a sinner.

Thy heart is My home; sanctify it for My descent.

I have made death a messenger of joy to thee. Wherefore dost thou grieve?

Make mention of Me on My earth, that in My heaven I may remember thee.

O rich ones on earth! The poor in your midst are My trust; guard ye My trust.

The source of all learning is the knowledge of God, exalted be His Glory.[7]

## *Do Bahá'ís believe in the afterlife?*

Bahá'ís regard this life as the first stage among infinite stages of our spiritual development. Here we prepare for another world, which we enter after death. The transition does not result in the loss of any of our spiritual powers: our intelligence, our individuality, and the memory of our lives here. In fact, it results in the gaining of new and greater spiritual powers.

The next world is far superior to this one, especially for those who have lived a noble life on this plane, who have pleased God. For them it is so splendid, so grand and enchanting that if they could experience it, they would no longer wish to continue to live. They would deem this world a dark and gloomy prison.

Bahá'u'lláh teaches that this realm is a place of planting, not harvesting; hence we should not always expect to receive the rewards of our good deeds here. He who plants a seed does not receive his harvest instantly. God wishes us to show our trust in Him by being patient.

> Because you have seen me, you have believed; blessed are those who have not seen and yet have believed.      Christ (John 20:29 NIV)

Bahá'u'lláh assures us that no act, however small, will be forgotten, that He who has made the universe can certainly preserve our deeds, and that our Creator is just and will not allow any act to go unrewarded.

Recent findings in the realm of near-death experience are in harmony with the Bahá'í teachings on this subject:

- Death does not destroy the self—its sense of individuality, identity, and consciousness.

- The soul enters a new spiritual dimension, indescribable in its beauty and perfection.

- Physical pain and infirmity (blindness, deafness, etc.) disappear.

- The soul gains new gifts and powers, like the freedom to travel throughout the universe without any instrument, and to pass through physical barriers.

- The soul remembers and reviews all the events of its life, including caring or uncaring acts.

- There is some kind of evaluation of one's life.

- The soul has a chance to meet his loved ones who have died.

- The soul encounters a spiritual being, who expresses unconditional love.

- The individual learns that the most splendid goal in life is to love and to learn.

Here are a few brief quotations from people with near-death visions:

> All pain vanished.
> I went through this dark, black vacuum at super speed.
> There was a feeling of utter peace and quiet, no fear at all.

After I came back, I cried off and on for about a week because I had to live in this world after seeing that one.

It opened up a whole new world for me...I kept thinking, 'There's so much that I've got to find out.'

I heard a voice telling me what I had to do—go back—and I felt no fear.[8]

## *Do Bahá'ís believe in heaven and hell?*

They do, but their interpretation differs from traditional views. Bahá'u'lláh teaches that heaven is a state of nearness to God and hell one of remoteness from Him. Heaven and hell are conditions that can exist both in this world and the next. Hell-fire is a state of being remote from God, the Source of all joys and perfections, and sensing a burning desire to attain His Presence.

Bahá'u'lláh further teaches that in the next realm our Creator provides opportunities for every soul to grow toward Him, even for those who have been full of evil thoughts and deeds. Since everyone will have this opportunity, those farthest from God in this life, will, in relation to others, continue to be farthest from Him in the next life.

As the womb is the place of preparation for this life, so is this life a place of preparation for the next. We should take advantage of every opportunity to attain the greatest possible spiritual growth.

After passing away from this realm we will not enjoy the unlimited opportunities that we have here. This world is a school. Our goal is to graduate with honor and distinction. The uniqueness of this life lies in this: it determines our eternal destiny.

The conditions of the next life are beyond our comprehension. It is futile to try to know exactly what will happen, or what it will be like. Sooner or later we will all make the journey. What we now need most is patience and trust.

## *Do Bahá'ís have priests?*

The Bahá'í community is directed by democratic methods. The functions of priests are performed by elected assemblies at the local and national levels. The Universal House of Justice, also an elected body, coordinates and directs the Bahá'í community at the international level.

Prophecies declare that everything will be made new "at the end of the age." The Bahá'í social order is so new that it cannot be compared with any other existing social order. Its success in fostering and protecting the unity and harmony of the Bahá'í community—and moving it forward toward a glorious goal, through the most noble means—presents one more evidence of its distinction and divine origin. The present Bahá'í community, which encompasses over 200 countries and territories, offers a perfect model for the future world order, when all humanity will acknowledge Bahá'u'lláh's revelation.

## *How does the Bahá'í Faith differ from Christianity?*

Teaching should always be adapted to the learner. Christ spoke to people living in a simple world. Since His time the world has steadily grown more complex. What worked then may not work now.

As a child needs new guidance at each stage of his development, so does the human race. God has a plan and purpose for us, which He reveals progressively, through His Messengers and Redeemers, according to our needs and maturity. The Bahá'í Faith is the latest—but not the last—expression of that divine plan and purpose.

The truths taught by Christ have been expanded and adapted to our maturity. This is the difference between the Bahá'í Faith and Christianity.

## *What did Bahá'u'lláh say about Christ?*

He acknowledged and glorified Him in the most moving terms:

> Know thou that when the Son of Man yielded up His breath to God, the whole creation wept with a great weeping. By sacrificing Himself, however, a fresh capacity was infused into all created things. Its evidences, as witnessed in all the peoples of the earth, are now manifest before thee. The deepest wisdom which the sages have uttered, the profoundest learning which any

mind hath unfolded, the arts which the ablest hands have produced, the influence exerted by the most potent of rulers, are but manifestations of the quickening power released by His transcendent, His all-pervasive, and resplendent Spirit.

We testify that when He [Christ] came into the world, He shed the splendor of His glory upon all created things. Through Him the leper recovered from the leprosy of perversity and ignorance. Through Him, the unchaste and wayward were healed. Through His power, born of Almighty God, the eyes of the blind were opened, and the soul of the sinner sanctified.[9]

### *When a person accepts the Bahá'í Faith, what happens to his previous beliefs?*

The Bahá'í Faith is the fulfillment of all the world's religions. When a seed is planted, it grows into many parts and forms, but all the forms originate from the same seed and are expressions of the same potential. Each part has a different name: branch, leaf, flower, and fruit. But all parts grow from the same single seed.

Similarly, each of the world's great religions, though unique and seemingly different from all the others, is in essence an expression of the same Creative Power. By acknowledging *other* faiths, instead of *losing* our faith, we *expand* it; we gain new knowledge and awareness.

The teachings of the great religions stand as bright candles lit from time to time by the Hands of the Light Bringers—God's great Messengers and Redeemers. As we acknowledge each candle, we add to our enlightenment, to our understanding of truth; we see more distinctly the divine purpose, the wondrous path of human destiny.

Since each religion relates to the needs and potential of the people of its time, the knowledge offered by the latest revelation must necessarily transcend that offered by previous revelations; it must harmonize more intimately with its recipients' potential and needs, their nature and aspirations. In this lies the strength of the Bahá'í Faith. By being the latest of the great revelations, it relates fully to *our* potential, *our* needs, *our* time, and *our* temperament.

## *Why do people accept the Bahá'í Faith?*

Despite many obstacles, the Bahá'í Faith has become a universal faith. It is now the second most widely spread religion in the world. Further, the rate of the spread of the Bahá'í Faith has been accelerating from its very beginning. The light of Bahá'u'lláh is so dazzling that it attracts enlightened believers and seekers from all walks of life, from all religions and cultures. The following are a few reasons why, despite the obstacles, so many people have turned to the Bahá'í Faith as the religion that God has destined for our time:

- They find the Bahá'í Faith to be the fulfillment of all the scriptural prophecies.

- They find a religion that they can practice. They see harmony between their beliefs and their actions.

- They discover that the Bahá'í Faith is built on enlightened faith, not dogma.

- They see harmony between their religious beliefs and scientific knowledge.

- They learn that God is the God of love, reason, and mercy—not of fear, anger, and revenge.

- They find a religion that strengthens their family relations and provides clear moral standards for their children.

- They find satisfactory answers to their unresolved questions, for the Bahá'í Faith offers a rational approach to religion.

- They learn that they can make a difference, that they can create a better world, instead of just talking about its problems.

- As a result of the spiritual strength they gain, they experience far fewer conflicts.

- They gain a sense of peace and joy that they have not known before.

- They find the Bahá'í community to be diverse yet united.

- They gain friends who practice high ethical standards.

- They find that their love for God and humankind grows stronger.
- They find that the Bahá'í Faith crowns their life with hope, a bright hope for their future as well as for the world. They gain a glowing and eternal purpose.

Many people search ardently for happiness. They look everywhere except where it lies in abundance. There are millions of Bahá'ís who will admit to having been quite skeptical about most or all of the blessings listed here. They will also acknowledge that, to their surprise, their skepticism faded away when they saw Bahá'ís living the Bahá'í life.

Observing how the followers of a faith live is the ultimate test of that faith. Their ideals and their actions are the fruits of the religion that they follow.

> By their fruit you will recognize them. Do people pick grapes from thornbushes, or figs from thistles? Likewise every good tree bears good fruit, but a bad tree bears bad fruit. A good tree cannot bear bad fruit, and a bad tree cannot bear good fruit.      Christ (Matt. 7:16-18 NIV)

## *Should everyone investigate the Bahá'í Faith?*

The Bahá'í Faith is not just for Christians and Jews. It is for the entire human race. All sacred Scriptures have foretold the advent of a great Redeemer in our time:

> All the…Books of God are adorned with His
> praise and extol His glory.[10]    Bahá'u'lláh

Every human being has a spiritual obligation to test
the validity of Bahá'u'lláh's mission. Sometimes
we make decisions simply on the basis of unverified assumptions. Eventually we learn the consequence of such decisions. As a rule the consequence
comes too late to repair the damage. We are told
that every decision (good or bad) has only short-
lived results except those that affect the state of our
soul, those that determine our relationship with
God. Such decisions must be taken more seriously
than any others, yet most people take them very
lightly, less than the most trivial decisions of their
lives such as buying a toothbrush. They investigate
the toothbrush but not the truth. Even if someone
chose an unsuitable profession, it would not matter
much. For death brings to an end everything except
the spiritual state of the soul.

If we ignore God's guidance, our souls remain in
despair and darkness. God's guidance is the light
of our inner life.

> He that was hidden from the eyes of men is
> revealed, girded with sovereignty and power!…
> O ye that inhabit the heavens and the earth!
> There hath appeared what hath never previous-
> ly appeared. He Who, from everlasting, had
> concealed His Face from the sight of creation is
> now come.[11]    Bahá'u'lláh

> Seize the time, therefore, ere the glory of the
> divine springtime hath spent itself, and the Bird

of Eternity ceased to warble its melody, that thy inner hearing may not be deprived of hearkening unto its call. This is My counsel unto thee and unto the beloved of God. Whosoever wisheth, let him turn thereunto; whosoever wisheth, let him turn away. God, verily, is independent of him and of that which he may see and witness.[12]

Bahá'u'lláh

And the Spirit and the bride say, Come. And let him that heareth say, Come. And let him that is athirst come. And whosoever will, let him take the water of life freely.     Christ (Rev. 22:17)

## *How does one become a Bahá'í?*

Becoming a Bahá'í is as simple and yet as difficult as acknowledging that Bahá'u'lláh is God's Messenger and Redeemer for this age, and trying to practice His laws and teachings. This does not require any ceremony. In most countries, when someone wishes to join the Bahá'í Faith, he signs a card, which serves as the symbol of his spiritual commitment.

✷ ✷ ✷

But at that time your people—everyone whose name is found written in the book—will be delivered…Those who are wise will shine like the brightness of the heavens…     Daniel 12:1-3 NIV

Whoso hath, in this Day, refused to allow the doubts and fancies of men to turn him away from Him Who is the Eternal Truth, and hath not suffered [allowed]…the ecclesiastical [religious] and secular authorities to deter him from recognizing His Message, such a man will be regarded by God, the Lord of all men, as one of His mighty signs, and will be numbered among them whose names have been inscribed by the Pen of the Most High in His Book. Blessed is he that hath recognized the true stature of such a soul, that hath acknowledged its station, and discovered its virtues.[13]                      Bahá'u'lláh

# Part II

## *Bahá'u'lláh*
## The Glory of God

A purpose of this series is to introduce *Bahá'u'lláh—the Glory of God*—to the western world. He is the One promised in all Scriptures. He has come to establish the heavenly Kingdom both within our soul and without. Only once in a thousand years a spiritual Figure, a Messenger and Redeemer from God, such as Bahá'u'lláh appears upon the earth. You now have a chance to know Him, to get a glimpse of His glory—a glory that will in time fill the earth:

> For the earth will be filled with the knowledge of *the glory of the Lord*, as the waters cover the sea.
>
> Habakkuk 2:14 NIV

> …all the earth shall be filled with *the glory of the Lord*.　　Numbers 14:21

# Who Was Bahá'u'lláh?

In examining the evidence for the One who has claimed to speak the Word of God, the most vital questions are these: Who was He? What was He like? How did He live? What happened to Him? Here are a few features of Bahá'u'lláh's life, adapted mostly from a book entitled *Some Answered Questions*:

Bahá'u'lláh was born in 1817, in Persia, to a rich and noble family. He died in 1892, as a prisoner and exile in the Holy Land. As an infant, He astonished His parents by His uniqueness and distinctions. His father related that He would never cry or scream. "You don't know," he said, "what a potential He has, how intelligent He is! He is like a flame of fire, and in His tender years superior to young people." [1] Bahá'u'lláh's father was so captivated by Him that he wrote a piece of poetry in his son's honor, inscribed it on a plaque, and hung it on the wall of a summer mansion in which Bahá'u'lláh lived. The content of the poetry shows that the father sensed the divine destiny of his Son:

> When thou enterest the sacred abode of the Beloved say:
>
> "I am at thy command.
>
> This is the home of love; enter with reverence.
>
> This is holy ground; remove thy shoes when thou enterest here."[2]

People were attracted by Bahá'u'lláh's many distinctions. He did not attend any school, yet astonished people by His wisdom and knowledge. Even His enemies testified to His greatness. Great thinkers flocked to His presence, asking Him their most difficult questions. They said, "This man is unique in all perfections."

> He had an extraordinary power of attraction, which was felt by all. People always crowded around Him. Ministers and people of the Court would surround Him, and the children also were devoted to Him. When He was only thirteen or fourteen years old He became renowned for His learning. He would converse on any subject and solve any problem presented to Him. In large gatherings He would…explain intricate religious questions. All of them used to listen to Him with the greatest interest.[3]

He showed no interest in politics:

> When Bahá'u'lláh was twenty two years old, His father died, and the Government wished

Him to succeed to His father's position in the Ministry…but Bahá'u'lláh did not accept the offer. Then the Prime Minister said: "Leave him to himself. Such a position is unworthy of him. He has some higher aim in view. I cannot understand him, but I am convinced that he is destined for some lofty career. His thoughts are not like ours. Let him alone."[4]

Bahá'u'lláh was known especially for His generosity and love for the poor:

He was most generous, giving abundantly to the poor. None who came to Him were turned away. The doors of His house were open to all.[5]

One day Bahá'u'lláh sent 'Abdu'l-Bahá, His eldest Son, to inspect the work of the shepherds who were taking care of His sheep. 'Abdu'l-Bahá was a small child at the time, and the persecutions against Bahá'u'lláh and His family had not yet started. Bahá'u'lláh then had a good deal of land in the mountains and owned large herds of sheep. When the inspection was finished and 'Abdu'l-Bahá was ready to leave, the man who had accompanied Him said, "It is your father's custom to leave a gift for each shepherd." 'Abdu'l-Bahá became silent for a while, because He did not have anything to give them. The man, however, insisted that the shepherds were expecting something. Then 'Abdu'l-Bahá had an idea that made Him very happy! He would give the shepherds the sheep they were taking care of! Bahá'u'lláh was very much pleased when He heard about

'Abdu'l-Bahá's generous thoughts towards the shepherds. He humorously remarked that everyone had better take good care of 'Abdu'l-Bahá because someday He would give Himself away. Of course, this is exactly what 'Abdu'l-Bahá did for the rest of His life. He gave everything He had, each and every moment of His life, to humanity, to unite us and bring us true happiness.[6]

Bahá'u'lláh was also known for His courage to stand against the powerful who would abuse their power:

All classes of men marveled at His miraculous success in emerging unscathed from the most perilous encounters. Nothing short of Divine protection, they thought, could have ensured His safety on such occasions…In His constant association, during those days, with the highest dignitaries of the realm…He was never content simply to accede to the views they expressed or the claims they advanced. He would, at their gatherings, fearlessly champion the cause of truth, would assert the rights of the downtrodden, defending the weak and protecting the innocent.[7]

Bahá'u'lláh spent the early part of His life in the utmost joy and happiness. But He later became a target of prejudice and persecution. Thousands of fanatical believers rose against Him. Religious leaders were terrified of losing their power. They said, "This man intends to destroy religion, law, the nation, and the empire." (People made the same accusations against Jesus.) He faced His enemies with the utmost courage, showing no weakness or fear.

Bahá'u'lláh endured nearly 40 years of imprisonment and exile, yet He never complained. No human being can imagine the extent of His sufferings. Among His sufferings was imprisonment in an infamous dungeon in Tihrán, known as the Black Pit or Black Dungeon, where He was kept for four months. In that dungeon He endured every conceivable pain and anguish:

- *Total darkness*: The underground prison had neither lights nor windows.

- *A terrible stench*: About 150 of the worst criminals were thrown in that dark, deep, and damp dungeon with no air circulation or sanitary facilities. The ground was covered with several inches of filthy mud and mire.

- *Hunger and thirst*: For the first three days and nights Bahá'u'lláh received neither food nor water.

- *Severe pain and lack of mobility*: Bahá'u'lláh's feet were put in stocks, and on His neck was placed a chain so heavy that He was unable to hold Himself upright. To hold the weight of the chain, Bahá'u'lláh had to press His hands against the ground covered with slime up to His wrists. From the weight of the harsh metal, His neck became inflamed and injured.

- *Little if any sleep*: Bahá'u'lláh could hardly sleep under those horrible conditions.

- *Lack of clothes*: His outer garments were stripped away on His way to the prison.

- ***Illness***: Because of the unsanitary conditions, Bahá'u'lláh suffered grave illness.

- ***Being poisoned***: He also suffered pain from consuming poison placed in His food.

- ***Homelessness***: All His properties were confiscated.

- ***Loneliness***: "During this time none of His friends were able to get access to Him."[8]

- ***Being surrounded by the worst criminals*** who had little if any hope of survival or freedom.

- ***Anxiety about His family***: Bahá'u'lláh's family members, including His young children, were left at the mercy of fanatical mobs, filled with rage and incited to seek revenge. (His Son, 'Abdu'l-Bahá, was then 9 years old.)

- ***Deep grief and concern for His devoted and distinguished disciples***, who were being hunted down, tortured, and killed by enraged mobs outside the prison.

- ***Concern about the future***: From that prison Bahá'u'lláh was banished to strange lands. As foretold in a prophecy (Matt. 25:41-46), He became a stranger (an exile). Never again did He see His homeland.

- ***Deep sorrow*** for those who were rejecting God's choicest blessings and bounties.*

---

* The Bible contains numerous prophecies that predict suffering for Jesus in His Second Advent. For a review of such prophecies, see ***King of Kings*** by this author.

It was in this dungeon that Bahá'u'lláh expressed the first intimations of His Divine Mission:

> One night, in a dream, these exalted words were heard on every side: "Verily, We shall render Thee victorious by Thyself and by Thy Pen. Grieve Thou not for that which hath befallen Thee, neither be Thou afraid, for Thou art in safety. Erelong will God raise up the treasures of the earth—men who will aid Thee through Thyself and through Thy Name..."[9]

Bahá'u'lláh repeatedly stated that He spoke only by God's command, and not of His own choosing. He declared:

> Think ye, O people, that I hold within My grasp the control of God's ultimate Will and Purpose? ...Had the ultimate destiny of God's Faith been in Mine hands, I would have never consented, even though for one moment, to manifest Myself unto you, nor would I have allowed one word to fall from My lips. Of this God Himself is, verily, a witness.[10]

> This is but a leaf which the winds of the will of thy Lord, the Almighty, the All-Praised, have stirred. Can it be still when the tempestuous winds are blowing? Nay, by Him Who is the Lord of all Names and Attributes![11]

Bahá'u'lláh's arrest and imprisonment in that dungeon give us only a glimpse of the sufferings He endured for nearly 40 years in three different countries. How could anyone survive the scourge of such unrelenting pressures? How much pain can a human being endure? Why would God allow the One He loved the most to go through so much suffering? Did not Jesus endure similar ordeals?

> Worldly friends, seeking their own good, appear to love one the other, whereas the true Friend [Bahá'u'lláh] hath loved and doth love you for your own sakes; indeed He hath suffered for your guidance countless afflictions. Be not disloyal to such a Friend, nay rather hasten unto Him.[12]
>
> Bahá'u'lláh

The religious leaders feared Bahá'u'lláh's influence, so they had Him exiled to another land. They thought in a strange land His influence would die out. But the result was that His charm captivated many more disciples. They exiled Him again and again. The results were the same—a spreading of His influence. Finally, they sent Him to the worst place they could find: a prison for murderers and thieves, located in a remote city ('Akká) with a dreadful climate and foul water. The sufferings Bahá'u'lláh endured in 'Akká surpassed even those He experienced in the Black Dungeon.

> Bahá'u'lláh was placed in a barren, filthy room, while His followers were crowded into another, the floor of which was covered with mud. Ten soldiers were posted to stand guard over them. To add further to their misery, the exiles, parched from a long day in the hot sun, soon found that the only water available to them was unfit for consumption. Mothers were unable to feed their babies, and infants cried for hours...

Under these conditions, all but 'Abdu'l-Bahá [Bahá'u'lláh's Son] and one other, fell ill. Within a matter of days three men died. The officials denied the prisoners permission to leave the citadel to bury them, and the guards demanded payment before removing the bodies. Bahá'u'lláh ordered that His prayer rug, the only item of any value that He possessed, be sold to cover the cost of the burial. The guards pocketed the money and buried the men in the clothes in which they died...

Three days after the exiles' arrival, the Sultán's edict was read aloud in the mosque. It sentenced Bahá'u'lláh, His family, and His companions to life imprisonment and expressly forbade the exiles to associate with one another or with local inhabitants.[13]

During Bahá'u'lláh's imprisonment in 'Akká, His young son was pacing the roof of the prison, "wrapped in devotions, when he fell through a skylight. Mortally wounded, his dying wish to his Father was that his life might be a ransom for those who were prevented from attaining Bahá'u'lláh's presence."[14] In a prayer, Bahá'u'lláh speaks of the sacrifice of His son:

I have, O my Lord, offered up that which Thou hast given Me, that Thy servants may be quickened, and all that dwell on earth be united.[15]

Here Bahá'u'lláh explains why He accepted so much pain and suffering:

The Ancient Beauty [Bahá'u'lláh] hath consented to be bound with chains that mankind may be released from its bondage, and hath accepted to be made a prisoner…that the whole world may attain unto true liberty. He hath drained to its dregs the cup of sorrow, that all the peoples of the earth may attain unto abiding joy, and be filled with gladness. This is of the mercy of your Lord, the Compassionate, the Most Merciful. We have accepted to be abased…that ye may be exalted, and have suffered manifold afflictions, that ye might prosper and flourish. He Who hath come to build anew the whole world, behold, how they...have forced Him to dwell within the most desolate of cities![16]

Despite this severe repression, Bahá'u'lláh's influence continued to spread, His glory became more evident. From behind prison walls, He triumphed over all His enemies.

For if this idea...is of human origin, it will collapse; but if it is from God, you will never be able to put them [the believers] down, and you risk finding yourself at war with God.

Acts 5:38-39

When Bahá'u'lláh was exiled to the Holy Land, those aware of biblical prophecies suddenly realized what had happened: Bahá'u'lláh's enemies had, unknowingly, become the very instruments for the fulfillment of prophecies about Him because the Bible predicts repeatedly that the Redeemer of the Last Days will come to the Holy Land. Those who had wished to destroy Him became the means of His triumph. (For a review of these prophecies and many others, see *I Shall Come Again, Lord of Lords,* and *King of Kings.*)

In 1868, while under arrest, Bahá'u'lláh addressed the kings and rulers of the earth, asking them to act with justice and to work for peace. With the exception of Queen Victoria, they ignored His call. He predicted their downfall and His own triumph.

Among these sovereigns was Napoleon III. Bahá'u'lláh asked him to investigate the reason for His imprisonment. The sovereign did not respond. Bahá'u'lláh sent a second letter, predicting his downfall. Soon thereafter, in 1870, war between Germany and France broke out. Everything seemed to be in Napoleon's favor, yet he was defeated, dishonored, and debased. According to *The Fall of Paris*:

> History knows of perhaps no more startling instance of what the Greeks called peripateia, the terrible fall from prideful heights. Certainly no nation in modern times, so replete with apparent grandeur and opulent in material achievement, has ever been subjected to a worse humiliation in so short a time.[17]

Other sovereigns addressed by Bahá'u'lláh encountered similar fates. Every prediction that Bahá'u'lláh made was fulfilled. These are discussed in a book titled *The Prisoner and the King*, by William Sears.

Bahá'u'lláh's greatness touched even those who did not follow Him. They wrote about His knowledge,

His kindness, and His patience. They flocked to His presence and marveled at His wondrous works.

How often would one of His bitter enemies say to himself, "When I see Him, I will argue with Him and defeat Him in this way..." But when faced with Bahá'u'lláh, he would find himself speechless—unable to utter a word.

Bahá'u'lláh declared His willingness to be tested. To leave the religious leaders with no excuse, Bahá'u'lláh said that He was willing to perform any miracle that they requested. The only condition He set was that, after the miracle was performed, they would acknowledge the validity of His claim. The religious leaders declined to accept the condition. (God has always refused requests to perform miracles to prove His power, see Matt. 4:7. We cannot be sure why Bahá'u'lláh accepted this request. Perhaps one reason was that He knew it would be rejected.)

Bahá'u'lláh demonstrated His dependence on the divine and detachment from worldly desires by associating with the poor and the humble and avoiding the powerful and the pompous.[18] A notable figure wanted to meet Bahá'u'lláh. But to be seen with Bahá'u'lláh meant danger. He sent a message asking to meet with Him secretly. In response, Bahá'u'lláh sent him a piece of poetry to this effect: "Unless you have a desire to sacrifice your life, don't come here. This is the way if you wish to meet Bahá. If you are unprepared for this journey, don't come, and don't bring trouble." The man dared not take the risk of endangering his life and declined.

For nearly 50 years Bahá'u'lláh faced bitter enemies who killed thousands of His followers, yet failed to destroy Him. Repeatedly they planned and plotted against Him, but to no avail.

Are these marks of distinction not similar to those found in the life of Jesus?

# Part III

# Wake Up! I Shall Come Upon You Like a Thief!

**Christ (Rev. 3:2-3 NEB)**

*An Invitation to Christians to Investigate the News of the Return of Christ*

Arise, shine, for *your light has come, and the glory of the Lord rises upon you*. See, darkness covers the earth and thick darkness is over the peoples, but the Lord rises upon you and his glory appears over you.     Isaiah 60:1-2 NIV

*Let the light of His glory*, O people, *shine upon you*, and be not of the negligent.[1]
    Bahá'u'lláh, The Glory of God

All the heavenly Scriptures of the past attest to the greatness of this Day, the greatness of this Manifestation, the greatness of His signs...Yet despite all this the people have remained heedless and are shut out as by a veil.[2]

Bahá'u'lláh, The Glory of God

This is the Day whereon the All-Merciful hath come down in the clouds of knowledge, clothed with manifest sovereignty.[3]

Bahá'u'lláh, The Glory of God

He Whose advent hath been foretold in the heavenly Scriptures is come, could ye but understand it. The world's horizon is illumined by the splendors of this Most Great Revelation. Haste ye with radiant hearts and be not of them that are bereft of understanding.[4]

Bahá'u'lláh, The Glory of God

Yea, the set time is come...for Jehovah hath appeared in His glory.

Psalms 102:13, 16 ARV

# Wake Up! I Shall Come Upon You Like a Thief!

## *Dawn of a New Day*

The light shines in the darkness, but the darkness has not understood it.                    John 1:5 NIV

The Dawn hath broken, yet the people understand not.[5]                    Bahá'u'lláh

The Dawn hath truly brightened and the light hath shone forth and the night hath receded. Happy are they that comprehend. Happy are they that have attained thereunto.[6]                    Bahá'u'lláh

## *God Speaks Again*

God's Plan is perfect. As soon as we are able to absorb more truth, He gives us more; as soon as something becomes irrelevant, He sends the relevant. Far be it from His wisdom, mercy, and justice to leave His children confused, hopeless, comfortless.

The necessity of the progressive revelation of truth not only appeals to the mind, it finds support in sacred Scriptures as well. For all Messengers prophesy the coming of other Messengers like themselves, who will bring still greater measures of knowledge and truth. In the following passage, Christ promises and predicts a further unfolding of truth in the future, when the receivers are ready:

> I have much more to say to you, more than you can now bear. But when he, the Spirit of truth, comes, he will guide you into all truth.
>
> Christ (John 16:12-13 NIV)

Who can fairly claim that, for the last century and a half, the world has not been ready for a new out-pouring of truth? Is not our Creator all-knowing? Does He not recognize our need for new truths, for new knowledge? Is He indifferent to our sorrows and our sufferings? In the words of Shoghi Effendi: "Who, contemplating the helplessness, the fears and miseries of humanity in this day, can any longer question the necessity for a fresh revelation of the quickening power of God's redemptive love and guidance?"[7]

## *Christ Returns*

> In this Day a great festival is taking place in the Realm above; for whatsoever was promised in the sacred Scriptures hath been fulfilled. This is the Day of great rejoicing. It behoveth everyone to hasten towards the court of His nearness with exceeding joy…and to deliver himself from the fire of remoteness.[8]     Bahá'u'lláh

The following song, often chanted in churches, is not a hope or a dream any more; it is reality: "Joy to the world the Lord is come!"

Bahá'u'lláh proclaims in the clearest, most certain, and most emphatic terms His Mission as the supreme Savior and Redeemer of all mankind, the Promised One of all ages and religions, the return of Christ to the Christians, and the Glory of the Lord to the followers of both the Torah and the Gospel. He claims a station referred to throughout the Scriptures as the Prince of Peace, the Return of the Son in the Glory of His Father, the Lord of the Vineyard, the Spirit of Truth, the Holy Spirit, the Comforter, the Counselor, and the King of Glory.

The following is a statement by Bahá'u'lláh proclaiming His Mission to all humanity:

> The time foreordained unto the peoples and kindreds of the earth is now come. The promises of God, as recorded in the holy Scriptures, have all been fulfilled. Out of Zion hath gone forth the Law of God, and Jerusalem, and the hills and land thereof, are filled with the glory of His Revelation. Happy is the man that pondereth in his heart that which hath been revealed in the Books of God, the Help in Peril, the Self-Subsisting. Meditate upon this, O ye beloved of God, and let your ears be attentive unto His Word, so that ye may, by His grace and mercy, drink your fill from the crystal waters of constancy, and become as steadfast and immovable as the mountain in His Cause.[9]

And this is a statement proclaiming His Mission specifically to Christians:

> Say, O followers of the Son [Jesus]! Have ye shut out yourselves from Me by reason of My

Name? Wherefore ponder ye not in your hearts? Day and night ye have been calling upon your Lord, the Omnipotent, but when He came from the heaven of eternity in His great glory, ye turned aside from Him...

Consider those who rejected the Spirit [Jesus] when He came unto them with manifest dominion. How numerous the Pharisees who had secluded themselves in synagogues in His name, lamenting over their separation from Him, and yet when the portals of reunion were flung open and the divine Luminary shone resplendent from the Dayspring of Beauty, they disbelieved in God, the Exalted, the Mighty. They failed to attain His presence, notwithstanding that His advent had been promised them in the Book of Isaiah as well as in the Books of the Prophets and the Messengers. No one from among them turned his face towards the Dayspring of divine bounty except such as were destitute of any power amongst men. And yet, today, every man endowed with power and invested with sovereignty prideth himself on His Name. Moreover, call thou to mind the one* who sentenced Jesus to death. He was the most learned of his age in his own country, whilst he who was only a fisherman

---

* Annas, the high priest, who declared that the death of Jesus was preferable to the death of the nation. Annas and Caiaphas were the highest ranking religious leaders of the Jews. They occupied the highest position of honor among those who professed faith in Judaism in their country, yet they became the highest symbol of denial, leading their followers to condemn Jesus to death.

believed in Him. Take good heed and be of them that observe the warning.[10]

And again:

We, verily, have come for your sakes, and have borne the misfortunes of the world for your salvation. Flee ye the One Who hath sacrificed His life that ye may be quickened? Fear God, O followers of the Spirit [the Christians], and walk not in the footsteps of every divine [religious leader] that hath gone far astray. Do ye imagine that He seeketh His own interests, when He hath, at all times, been threatened by the swords of the enemies; or that He seeketh the vanities of the world, after He hath been imprisoned in the most desolate of cities? Be fair in your judgment and follow not the footsteps of the unjust.[11]

## *False Prophets*

All sacred Scriptures warn against false prophets, against deceivers. Do the warnings intend to discourage search, to instill fear, to teach avoidance and indifference? Or do they intend to teach caution and prudence? For wide is the gap between fear and caution, between avoidance and prudence.

Our Creator wishes us to be critical: never accept anything without good reason. But He also wishes us to be daring and confident, never fear the truth.

Say to them that are of a fearful heart, be strong, fear not, behold, your God will come.

Isaiah 35:4

Fear implies avoiding or refusing to face reality. Being cautious or critical implies watching and responding with awareness. Fear says close your eyes, caution says keep them open and try to look objectively. Both extremes—being fearful and being credulous—deprive us from knowing the truth, stand as obstacles in our way. The virtue that can lead us to the object of our search is courage tempered with caution, confidence combined with prudence—not fear or avoidance.

To remain objective, we should rise above the accepted but fallacious notion that whatever we do not know, or do not believe in, or whatever is not accepted by a given majority, must necessarily be false. The verdict should come only when the search has been completed—not sooner. For it stands against justice to accuse someone with falsehood without giving him a hearing, before examining his claim or credentials. This is how Jesus, Moses, Abraham, Noah, and all the other great Teachers and Messengers were rejected by the masses and regarded as false prophets. People feared the truth, and they judged without searching. Should we not learn from their mistakes?

> Does our law condemn anyone without first hearing him…?                    John 7:51 NIV

## *Proofs of God's Word*

Truth can in no wise be confounded with aught else except itself; would that ye might ponder His proof. Nor can error be confused with Truth,

if ye do but reflect upon the testimony of God,
the True One.[12]                    The Báb (the Gate of God)
                                        Bahá'u'lláh's Herald

God never sends a Messenger without sustaining
His claim with clear and convincing proofs. It would
be far from His Justice to expect us to submit to
One who fails to demonstrate His supreme distinction clearly and convincingly, beyond any doubt; far
from His wisdom to expect us to follow One who
falls short of gleaming with unmatched glory, even
as a dazzling star in the midst of darkness, or as the
lightning which flashes forth from the East (Matt.
24:27). Bahá'u'lláh writes:

> The signs of God shine as manifest and resplen-
> dent as the sun amidst the works of His creatures.
> Whatsoever proceedeth from Him is apart, and
> will always remain distinguished, from the inven-
> tions of men. From the Source of His knowledge
> countless Luminaries of learning and wisdom
> have risen, and out of the Paradise of His Pen the
> breath of the All-Merciful hath continually been
> wafted to the hearts and souls of men. Happy
> are they that have recognized this truth.[13]

The first and the most relevant and reliable test of
the truth of a Revelator is His Revelation—the fruit
of His Self. To be effective, a test must be valid: it
must be relevant to the aim or the claim, the purpose
for which it is intended. A tree is best known by its
fruit, a flower by its fragrance. A physician can prove
his skill not by his mastery of pottery or poetry,
but by his healing powers. A divine Physician can

prove His claim and demonstrate His divine distinction not by astounding or amusing the curious crowds, but by manifesting His spiritual powers— His ability to elevate and ennoble the human spirit, His success in healing the spiritual maladies of mankind, in unifying and harmonizing human society, in raising a new culture and a new race of man. Such a strictly rational test of truth has been established and advocated in all sacred Scriptures. And it is one more evidence confirming harmony between science and religion, between reason and revelation.

## *I Shall Come Upon You Like a Thief (Rev. 3:3)*

Recently a study was made to assess people's beliefs about the afterlife. When asked "Do you believe hell really exists?" over 70 percent said: "Yes." But when asked "Do you believe you will go to hell?" only two percent said they believed that they would. What does this study say about human beings? One lesson it teaches us is this: We need to become a little more humble!

Based on the parable of the Banquet of the Kingdom (Matt. 25:1-13), Christians who fail to pay attention to the News of the Return of their Lord, Christians who are negligent in making an independent investigation of truth—even as a detective investigates a thief—will face a grim destiny. Contrary to their expectation, they will find that the door to the Kingdom of Heaven is closed to them.

The following dialogue portrays the destiny of negligent Christians and the way to avoid the prospect of facing a closed door:

> ***Negligent Christians plead with Jesus:*** "Sir! Sir! Open the door for us!"
>
> ***Jesus rejects their pleas by responding:*** "I do not know you."
>
> ***Jesus gives the reason for rejecting them:*** You were negligent in that you failed to "keep watch."
>
> ***To those who wish to face an open door Jesus declares:*** "Keep watch!"
>
> ***Jesus concludes by explaining why the believers should "watch:"*** "You do not know the day or the hour."

Question: Why would watching be required? For whom would we need to watch? For the one who comes from the sky, or for the one who comes like a thief?

Question: Why does "not knowing the day and the hour" necessitates watching? Because only if "the day and the hour" come and pass secretly will watching make any difference. That is why we are told:

- *I* shall come upon you like a thief (Rev. 3:3).

- The *day* of the Lord will come like a thief in the night (I Thess. 5:2).

Coming from the sky would not require any warnings. The warning (Be watchful! Be on guard!)

would be required only if the Advent was to be an ordinary event like the first one. Jesus lived like a thief among the Jews. They did not know who He was. Should we not learn a lesson from the way people behaved the first time?

## *The Greatness of This Day*

Ours is a most glorious day in human history; it is the day of the Lord (Isa. 25:9; Joel 2:31), the onset of the cycle of restoration and fulfillment (Acts 3:21), and the dawning of the divine Kingdom (Rev. 19:7; Rom. 15:12). It is an age glorified and extolled in all the Scriptures. Bahá'u'lláh declares again and again the uniqueness of our day:

> This is the Day in which God's most excellent favors have been poured out upon men, the Day in which His most mighty grace hath been infused into all created things. It is incumbent upon all the peoples of the world to reconcile their differences, and, with perfect unity and peace, abide beneath the shadow of the Tree of His care and loving-kindness.[14]

The Scriptures of all great religions refer again and again to a supreme Savior destined to inaugurate a new Universal Cycle in the spiritual evolution of humanity—a Savior extolled repeatedly throughout the Bible as the Glory of the Lord; referred to in the Gospel as the Spirit of Truth, the Lord of the Vineyard, the return of Christ; and in the Old Testament as the Lord, the Lord of Hosts, the King of Glory; a Redeemer destined to inaugurate for the first time in the spiritual evolution of humanity an era of lasting peace never broken by war; a period of prosperity never halted by poverty; an epoch of unity never divided by racial or national animosity; an age of light never followed by darkness; an era referred to as "the times of restitution [renewal and restoration] of all things, which God hath spoken by the mouth of all his holy prophets since the world began" (Acts 3:21), "the times of refreshing" (Acts 3:19), when all things are made new (Rev. 21:5).

Prior to the onset of the new cycle, humanity would have gone through the periods of infancy, childhood, and adolescence. It is only after this critical juncture (the end of the period of growth and the onset of maturity) that the Age of Peace and the Eden of Serenity and Tranquility would arrive. As the Scriptures attest:

> The sound of violence shall be heard no longer in your land, or ruin and devastation within your borders; but you shall call your walls Deliverance and your gates Praise. The sun shall no longer be your light by day, nor the moon shine on you when evening falls; the Lord shall be your everlasting light, your God shall be your glory. Never again shall your sun set nor your moon withdraw her light; but the Lord shall be your everlasting light and the days of your mourning shall be ended.  Isaiah 60:18-20 NEB

> There shall be no more night, nor will they need the light of lamp or sun, for the Lord God will give them light; and they shall reign for evermore.  Revelation 22:5 NEB

On that day men will say, See, this is our God
for whom we have waited to deliver us; this is
the Lord for whom we have waited; let us rejoice
and exult in his deliverance.        Isaiah 25:9 NEB

## *Independent Search for Truth*

Bahá'u'lláh does not wish anyone to accept Him
blindly, without first finding conclusive proofs of His
claim. But He does wish everyone to test His Faith
and His claim, and to test them by the strictest rules
of reason and according to specific standards set
forth in all the sacred Scriptures.

The Scriptures encourage us to examine every claim
and every "spirit" and to hold on to that which we
find noble and divine:

Do not put out the Spirit's fire; do not treat
prophecies with contempt. Test everything. Hold
on to the good.        I Thess. 5:19-21 NIV

By disregarding the prophecies, by ignoring the
divine Commandments to test the spirits (I John 4:1)
and to honor the truth, we stifle, without knowing,
the spreading of "the Spirit's fire"—a fire which
can set the world aflame:

I have come to set fire to the earth...
                    Christ (Luke 12:49 NEB)

Should all the servants read and ponder this,
there shall be kindled in their veins a fire that
shall set aflame the worlds.[15]        Bahá'u'lláh

The words of God have the power to enkindle every spirit. By disregarding the divine Words, by not setting our souls aflame, we restrain the spreading of the Fire of Faith—a Fire resplendent and divine, a Fire that can set aflame apathy, ignorance, gloom, fear, and despair; a force that can enkindle love, hope, peace, and harmony.

Every journey begins with a first step. A spiritual journey begins with an open, inquisitive, and thirsting mind. The Báb confirms the encouraging words of the Scriptures in similar terms. To discern the harmony of divine Words, let us review the words of the Scriptures, followed by those of the Báb:

> Do not put out the Spirit's fire; do not treat prophecies with contempt. Test everything. Hold on to the good.                    I Thess. 5:19-21 NIV

> Take heed to carefully consider the words of every soul, then hold fast to the proofs which attest the truth.[16]                    The Báb

## The Necessity of Following God's Standards

Our Creator not only asks us "to test the spirits, to see whether they are from God" (I John 4:1 NIV), whether they are divine or deceptive, He provides us with the testing tools as well. He designates the devices and the standards we should use in separating truth from falsehood. He gives us the "Touchstone of Divine Truth" and asks us to depend on It. How can we expect to find the truth, to separate the divine from the deceptive, if we use the wrong standards, if we depend on our own fantasies instead of the fundamental facts of the Scriptures? When we disregard the divine standards, we will fail in our efforts. We will fail even as a jeweler who, by using the wrong touchstone, falls short in appraising and cherishing a prized jewel.

As previously stated, our Creator declares again and again that we should try to know or judge His Saviors by their fruits—by what they produce, namely their lives, their teachings, their words, and their influence:

> A good tree cannot bear bad fruit, and a bad tree cannot bear good fruit...Thus, by their fruit you will recognize them.      Christ (Matt. 7:18,20 NIV)
> See also Luke 6:43-46; Mark 11:19; 12:33-34

How can we know or test the fruits without first tasting them? This booklet gives you your first taste of the fruits of the Vineyard of the Lord offered by the Lord of the Vineyard, your first glimpse of His divine glory and distinction.

## *The Consequences of Not Searching*

When people refuse to accept God's latest Revelation of Truth, when they try to live by the teachings of a faith whose time has passed and whose mission has been terminated, they cause much suffering for themselves and for others; they set in motion an unending cycle of strain and stress; they generate an aura of doubt and despair.

Bahá'ís believe that the multitudes of problems afflicting humanity today stem from the refusal of the masses to acknowledge the Redeemer for this age. And as long as the refusal persists, so will the problems. For human solutions are inadequate to solve spiritual problems. Only the divine Remedy can heal the spiritual maladies of humanity.

When outdated solutions are applied to modern problems, everyone suffers, especially those who live on hope for a better world and a brighter future, namely the youth. When those in positions of authority fail to provide guidance, it is the youth who must carry the greatest burden of their failure, and the greatest weight of uncertainty, doubt, and confusion.

Youth rank high when it comes to such attributes as curiosity and sense of wonder and adventure. They are quick to see discrepancies, to take notice of hypocrisy, irrationalism and irrelevance, and to question what others accept on blind faith. And when they are asked to submit to doctrines or dogmas that they find impractical, irrational, or irrelevant, they rebel not only against the dogmas but against religion itself. If this process is allowed to continue, rebellion against religion will become so massive and so intense as to lead to the total eclipse of faith. This is why it is so essential to bring the new Revelation into the life of the masses of humanity, especially the youth, while there is yet time—before Hope has grown too dim to be reignited, before Faith has been fully smothered and extinguished in the heart of the world.

## *God's Covenant With Humanity*

> The Lord of the universe hath never raised up a prophet nor hath He sent down a Book unless He hath established His covenant with all men, calling for their acceptance of the next Revelation and of the next Book; inasmuch as the outpourings of His bounty are ceaseless and without limit.[17]                                        The Báb

We are bound to our Creator by a covenant of reciprocity. This covenant clarifies our relationship with God, which is based on both justice and grace. The very gifts and potentials that God has granted to us require a response, an appreciation expressed both in words and deeds. Whether we like it or not, by receiving the gift of life we enter into a covenant with our Creator to abide by certain rules or laws. By doing our share we simply say: thanks for the gifts. Would it be seemly to ignore, dislike, or reject our loving and wise parents who have given us of their best? The same rule applies to us in our relationship to God.

At no time are we forced to live by the covenant. We are only asked, encouraged, and sometimes warned of the consequences of ignoring or rejecting the covenant. We are told:

> ...if ye believe not, ye yourselves will suffer.[18]
> Bahá'u'lláh

The covenant is very fair. It simply states: to the extent that you live by the rules, so are you entitled to the gifts.

Now how can we fulfill our side of the covenant? First, we must accept the Teacher that God has sent for our time; and second, we must obey the teachings of that Teacher. Following God's Commandments is the surest way of saying: we love you and trust you.

## The Three Stages of the Spiritual Evolution of Humanity

The Bahá'í teachings reveal that humanity must pass through three stages or periods of evolution:

## 1

### The Age of Prophecy

This is the period of preparation and anticipation extending over the past history of humanity.

## 2

### The Age of Transition

This is the period of transition from promise to fulfillment, the stage of cleansing-and-building. It started with the advent of the Báb in 1844 and will continue to the onset of the Golden Age, when righteousness shall reign, justice abound, and peace prevail. This period of transition is referred to in the Scriptures as the last day, the latter days, or the end of the age, meaning the last or latter days of preparation and anticipation, and the ending of the age of immaturity.

# 3

## *The Golden Age*

Following our age—the age of transition or preparation—will arrive the final phase in the evolution of mankind, the era of fulfillment and maturity. This is the time when the New Order is embraced, "the Most Great Justice" is realized, and the promised Kingdom is established with full glory and splendor.

The oppressions of our age are paving the way for the onset of the golden age. Bahá'u'lláh predicts:

> These great oppressions [that have befallen the world]...are preparing it for the advent of the Most Great Justice.[19]

And again:

> Bestir yourselves, O people, in anticipation of the days of Divine justice, for the promised hour is now come. Beware lest ye fail to apprehend its import...[20]

The strain and stress of our time are but the pangs of pain preceding the auspicious birth of a new civilization, a heavenly and glorious culture. Bahá'u'lláh declares:

> The whole earth...is now in a state of pregnancy. The day is approaching when it will have yielded its noblest fruits, when from it will have sprung forth the loftiest trees, the most enchanting blossoms, the most heavenly blessings. The time is approaching when every created thing will have

cast its burden. Glorified be God Who hath vouchsafed this grace that encompasseth all things, whether seen or unseen![21]

And again:

Soon will the present-day order be rolled up, and a new one spread out in its stead. Verily, thy Lord speaketh the truth, and is the Knower of things unseen.[22]

The world's equilibrium hath been upset through the vibrating influence of this most great, this new World Order. Mankind's ordered life hath been revolutionized through the agency of this unique, this wondrous System—the like of which mortal eyes have never witnessed.[23]

The *Book of Revelation* clearly predicts the passing away of the old order and the coming of the new:

I heard a loud voice proclaiming from the throne: "Now at last God has his dwelling among men! He will dwell among them and they shall be his people, and God himself will be with them. He will wipe every tear from their eyes; there shall be an end to…crying and pain; for *the old order has passed away*!"     Revelation 21:3-4 NEB

## *Our Role in This Critical Phase in Human History*

Our era coincides with the second phase: the building-and-cleansing period. As the old world order is crumbling, a new one is being built to replace it. Bahá'u'lláh predicts, "The day is approaching when We will have rolled up the world and all that is therein, and spread out a new order in its stead. He, verily, is powerful over all things."[24]

At present, Bahá'ís living in more than 200 countries and dependencies are working to make this prayer and this promise a reality:

> Our Father which art in heaven, Hallowed be thy name. Thy kingdom come. Thy will be done in earth, as it is in heaven.     Christ (Matt. 6:9-10)

Ours is the most critical era in human history. We are privileged with the unequaled honor of building a new civilization planned by the Creator Himself, a glorious Kingdom promised by all the great Messengers "since the world began," a reign destined to last as long as man himself. Yes, ours is the honor of being the pioneers in this great spiritual adventure, the builders of this heavenly and wondrous world, this divine and peerless Order. In the words of Bahá'u'lláh:

> Seize your chance…inasmuch as a fleeting moment in this Day excelleth centuries of a bygone age...Neither sun nor moon hath witnessed a day such as this...It is evident that every age in which a Manifestation of God hath lived is divinely ordained and may, in a sense, be characterized as God's appointed Day. This Day, however, is unique and is to be distinguished from those that have preceded it.[25]

And in the words of Bahá'u'lláh's Herald, the Báb:

Assuredly we are today living in the Days of God. These are the glorious days on the like of which the sun hath never risen in the past. These are the days which the people in bygone times eagerly expected.[26]

As the night fades away and the dawn nears, there occurs a mingling of light and darkness—a brief interval characterized by both anticipation and confusion. This is our time. Then gradually the splendors of the sun triumph—slowly but steadily—over the last lingering traces of darkness, reigning unhindered with dazzling brightness, crowned with unexcelled glory and grandeur. We are accorded the unequaled honor of witnessing the dawn of this great Day of the Lord rising steadily and confidently as the last citadels of darkness fall:

The morning cometh, and also the night...

Isaiah 21:12

The light shines in the darkness, but the darkness has not understood it.      John 1:5 NIV

O peoples of the earth! Verily the resplendent Light of God hath appeared in your midst, invested with this unerring Book, that ye may be guided aright to the ways of peace and, by the leave of God, step out of the darkness into the light and onto this far-extended Path of Truth.[27]      The Báb

Come, let us go up to the mountain of the Lord …Come…let us **walk in the light of the Lord**.

Isaiah 2:3-5 NIV

Arise thou to serve the Cause of thy Lord; then give the people the joyful tidings concerning this resplendent Light whose revelation hath been announced by God through His Prophets and Messengers.[28]        Bahá'u'lláh

O son of man! The light hath shone on thee... Wherefore, free thyself from the veils of idle fancies and enter into My court, that thou mayest be fit for everlasting life and worthy to meet Me. Thus may death not come upon thee, neither weariness nor trouble.[29]        Bahá'u'lláh

Blessed are those who have learned to acclaim you, who walk in the light of your presence...
        Psalms 89:15 NIV

By the righteousness of God! The Dawn hath truly brightened and the light hath shone forth and the night hath receded. Happy are they that comprehend. Happy are they that have attained thereunto.[30]        Bahá'u'lláh

O My servants! Deprive not yourselves of the unfading and resplendent Light that shineth within the Lamp of Divine glory. Let the flame of the love of God burn brightly within your radiant hearts.[31]        Bahá'u'lláh

Seize ye the living waters of immortality in the name of your Lord, the Lord of all names, and drink ye in the remembrance of Him, Who is the Mighty, the Peerless.[32]        Bahá'u'lláh

# Part IV

## Proofs of the Bahá'í Faith

*How can we know, and be absolutely certain, that Bahá'u'lláh is the True One—a Messenger from God—the One promised in all Scriptures?*

*Let us reason together, sayeth the Lord.*
*Isaiah 1:18*

# Choosing Your Destiny

"Where do we come from? What on earth are we doing? And where are we going?" These questions have been debated since the dawn of history. Some people support the earthly view. They think we evolved from bacteria and at death return to them in a "grave condition" to pay back our debts and sustain their survival! Others cherish the heavenly view, expressed in these words and verses:

> *Verily, we are God's, and to Him shall we return.[1]*
> *Bahá'u'lláh*

> *Behold, all souls are Mine.*        *Ezekiel 18:4*

> *The spirit shall return unto God.*  *Ecclesiastes 12:7*

To become worthy of the honor of returning to our Creator and attaining His presence, we must set our heart and soul on one goal: the cultivation of our spiritual potential. That is the prime purpose of our lives. We are not cells in aging bodies, but eternal souls set on an ever-advancing journey towards the One who made us. Can a traveler who stands still reach his destination? Our destination is God; the path that can lead us to His presence is paved with spiritual purity and perfection.

Which one is the master? The body or the soul? Devoting our precious lives to the demands of the flesh is spiritual slavery. It is laboring without reward. It is wasting the precious days of our lives.

We are told that our everlasting destiny is determined by the choices we make during our brief journey on earth. Some choices are trivial; others lead to far-reaching—indeed everlasting—consequences. Among the thousands, perhaps millions, of choices we make and actions we take during our lifetime, which ones count the most in shaping our destiny and leading us towards God—our ultimate goal? Can any choice or action be as critical and far-reaching as the following:

- *Knowing, loving, and trusting God*
- *Discovering what He has planned for each of us, and*
- *Taking action to fulfill that plan.*

## *Discovering God's Plan for Each of Us*

Is there a roadmap that can lead us to our destination, that can disclose what God has planned for each of us? To discover the answer to this question, we must consider this universal principle: ***To succeed in a task, we must meet certain requirements***. Is the glorious task of accomplishing our spiritual mission an exception to this rule? Can we reach this goal without making some effort, without meeting certain requirements? What are those rules or requirements?

After much suffering, Job answered God and said:

> My ears had ***heard*** of you, but now my eyes have ***seen*** you. Job 42:1, 5

What Job experienced holds true with everyone. In our journey toward God, we face and must pass through the same stages:

- The stage of "***hearing***"
- The stage of "***seeing***"

What do we need to accomplish during the first stage—that of "***hearing***?"

1. We must first discover the latest Revelation of divine knowledge: the religion that God has sent specifically for our time. Because only the latest religion provides the most timely instructions and the most relevant roadmap guiding us towards our divine destiny, towards what God has planned for each of us and for the world. Can the instructions we received in the first grade be adequate when we are in the 12th grade?

2. We must then carefully study the teachings of that religion—the latest Revelation of Guidance from God to humankind.

If you have read this book up to this point, you have already fulfilled—although on a small scale—the preceding requirements. You have already passed through the "***stage of hearing***."

To reach the final destination, ***you must also pass through the "stage of seeing."*** That requires you to take three additional steps:

1. ***Study the life of the One who has established the latest Revelation from God***. The Tree of Life—can be recognized not only by its fruit but also by the life of ***the One who planted it***.

2. ***Study the sacred Scriptures of that Revelation***. The sacred Scriptures of a Revelation are its heart and soul. They are the fruits of the Tree of Life.

3. ***Examine the prophecies that it has fulfilled***. Prophecies are the roots of the Tree of Life.

What then is the difference between "***hearing***" and "***seeing***"? Each of them points to a different degree or dimension of certainty. You may doubt the truth of something you ***hear***, but can you doubt the truth of something you ***see***? During ***the first*** stage of your search—that of "***hearing***"—you are able to taste ***the fruits*** of the Bahá'í Faith—the most recent Revelation from God—to discover the answer to this question: Is the Bahá'í Faith a ***fruitful*** Tree planted by the divine hand, or is it a ***fruitless*** tree planted by a deceptive plotter. Note how Jesus clarified this question:

> Do people pick grapes from thornbushes, or figs from thistles? Likewise every good tree bears good fruit, but a bad tree bears bad fruit. ***A good tree cannot bear bad fruit, and a bad tree cannot bear good fruit***. Every tree that does not

bear good fruit is cut down and thrown into the
fire. Thus, by their fruit you will recognize them.

Christ (Matt. 7:16-20 NIV)

During the **second** stage of your journey—that of
**seeing**—you will discover the answer to these
questions:

- Is the Bahá'í Faith rooted in God's Wisdom
  and Authority? **Does the life of Bahá'u'lláh
  manifest the divine distinctions?**

- **Are His Words the Word of God?** Did He
  speak them on His own authority, or was He
  a spokesman for the One who inspired Him
  to speak?

- **Is the Bahá'í Faith the fulfillment of the
  promises made in all the sacred Scriptures
  of the past?** Is it rooted in the Bible?

Surely the Sovereign Lord does nothing without
revealing his plan to his servants the prophets.

Amos 3:7 NIV

Blessed is the one who reads the words of this
prophecy, and blessed are those who hear it and
take to heart what is written in it.

Revelation 1:3 NIV

*When you pass through the "stage of seeing" your
certainty rises to a level scientists call "the critical
mass," where all your doubts disappear*. You will
no longer consider the Bahá'í Faith only as a great
idea that may create a better world; you will begin
to see it as the greatest and most glorious revelation
of divine knowledge to humankind. You will no

longer consider Bahá'u'lláh simply as a progressive thinker, a leader, a philosopher or a genius, but the One who holds the blueprint to transform our entire planet into a place of peace. You will no longer regard the Bahá'í Faith as just one more Faith or denomination among hundreds of others, but a Faith that manifests to perfection God's Authority and Wisdom. You will recognize it as a Revelation that provides a Plan, not only for humankind as a whole, but also as a roadmap for *your* life and the life of every other person for the next thousand years and more.

When you pass through the "*stage of seeing*" you reach the crest of certainty. You rise above the clouds that may prevent you from seeing the sun. Can anyone who sees the sun, deny its glory and grandeur?

> *The signs of God shine as manifest and resplendent as the sun amidst the works of His creatures.[2]*          Bahá'u'lláh

> *[A true seeker] will discriminate between truth and falsehood, even as he doth distinguish the sun from shadow.[3]*          Bahá'u'lláh

During the *first* phase of your journey, you will enter the heavenly Mansion, enjoy its beauty and grandeur, but later, because of tests and trials, you many change your mind and leave. The *second* phase does not allow for a change of mind. Once you enter that phase, you become a resident of the Mansion. Living within and serving becomes the very purpose of your life.

While you are passing through the "***stage of seeing***:"

- You learn to trust God and welcome what He is planned for you.

- You discover that the world is a friendly place, and that during your journey on earth you have a critical role to play.

- You learn that the things that cause pain and suffering are only small bumps on the road to a life of abundant joy and peace.

- You become highly motivated to make the greatest difference while you have a chance. You become supremely conscious of these urgent reminders:

*Teach us to count how few days we have and so gain wisdom of heart.*            ***Psalms 90:12***

*Seize thy chance, for it will come to thee no more.[4]*            ***Bahá'u'lláh***

*Imperishable glory I have chosen for thee… While there is yet time, return, and lose not thy chance.[5]*            ***Bahá'u'lláh***

When you pass through the "***stage of seeing***" you come to this conclusion: "In no way can I cultivate my spiritual potential and fulfill my divine destiny without stepping into the light of the new Knowledge manifested in this age through ***Bahá'u'lláh— the Glory of God***.

## The Role of Reason
## in Religion

In discovering what God has planned for us, should we submit to the dictates of emotions, or depend on the demands of reason? What is a reliable standard? The validity of religion, like science, must stand on evidence; if it cannot pass the test of reason, it should be rejected. Any seeker who investigates the truth of a religion must demand proofs. If a religion cannot prove itself, it is unworthy of attention. What a different world it would be if all people followed this one rule, if they demanded irrefutable evidence for the truth of a religion before believing in it?

The prime reason science moves forward is this: scientists do not depend on what their parents or friends tell them to believe. They demand evidence. What has been, and still is, the norm in religion? Ask a hundred people: "Why are you a Christian, a Jew, or a Muslim?" What do you think they will say? If they followed the rules of reason, as scientists do, would they not be following one harmonious system of beliefs?

## The Difference Between
## Divine and Deceptive

We all reflect on this question: Is it easy to tell the difference between the divine and the deceptive? Ponder for a moment, and ask yourself: Can there be a comparison between what God plans and what a deceiver devises? Would they not be as different as light and darkness? Can anyone with open eyes mistake one for the other?

As long as people fail to demand evidence for their beliefs, two things will happen:

- *Deceivers will continue to find receptive listeners.*

- *The followers of great religions will remain divided.*

You now have a chance and a choice to reverse both of these trends by doing exactly what others fail to do: demand convincing proofs for the truth of the Bahá'í Faith. If you fail to find such proofs, then reject it without hesitation.

The purpose for including this section is to encourage you to move forward in your journey in the search for truth, to help you become aware that the Bahá'í Faith does not consist merely of grand principles, and lofty goals and teachings.

The Bible compares a new Revelation to "the Tree of Life" (Rev. 22:2, 14). In what way are they comparable? And what are the main parts of this tree? To recognize a true religion, we must seek knowledge. Can we learn the mysteries of science without studying it? To reach a state of absolute certainty, not only we must examine the Tree but also study the life of the One who planted it. We should investigate all the following:

*Fruits:*    **The fruits of the Tree of Life are its Scriptures and teachings**.

*Leaves:*    **The leaves of this celestial Tree are the transforming and healing powers it generates in the spiritual life of the believers.**

*Trunk:*    **The trunk of this blessed Tree is its divine institutions**.

*Roots:*    **The roots of this heavenly Tree are the prophecies it has fulfilled**.

*Gardener:*    **The Gardener is the Founder of the new Faith—the One who owns and plants the Tree of Life.**

The books introduced later (see ***Part VI***) cover all the preceding features. They demonstrate that the Bahá'í Faith is indeed a heavenly Tree—so mighty and so deeply rooted in the Bible and other sacred Scriptures—that only God, the divine Gardener, could have planted and preserved it.

Just as religion is "***the Tree of Life***," so is our faith, which must bear not only luscious fruits, but also be rooted in reason—in the Word of God, and in the prophecies. Those who accept a religion without demanding evidence may compromise their own spiritual destiny. They may allow the clouds of emotions and illusions, rather than the light of reason and wisdom, to be their guide. Without knowing:

- They may ***accept a false religion***
- They may ***reject a true religion***

What is the most distinctive mark of being human? What quality separates us from animals? Our ability to think, to reason, and to understand. Imagine the consequences of failing to use these powers! Yet how few people depend on them as a guide to their everlasting destiny!

Why did God give us the gift of reasoning? Is it not for recognizing the truth, for discovering the purpose of our lives? What if we fail to depend on this gift? Would we not be in the position of a traveler who tries to find a house without an address or directions?

If you take the time to read some of the books introduced in the next section, you will be rewarded in two ways:

- *You will discover that the evidence for the divine origin of the Bahá'í Faith is as compelling as the evidence for scientific laws.*

- *Once you fully accept the Bahá'í Faith, you will not waver in your belief. Your rational powers will prevent you from denying the truth, even as these same powers prevent you from denying the established laws of science.*

## *Taking Time for Your Eternal Destiny*

We do not come to this world to "make a living." "Making a living" is not an end, but a means to an end: gaining the most glorious Gift that God may bestow on humans. What is that Gift? It is the gift of "***spiritual life***"—a life that will last as long as eternity. Can we gain this most precious Gift without an effort?

The world is demanding. It consumes all our energies and asks for more. If ***we*** fail to set priorities, ***the demands of the day*** will set our priorities for us. Even 15 minutes a day devoted to our spiritual destiny can transform the quality of our life in ways we cannot imagine. "Let us reason together, says the Lord" (Isa. 1:18). While at high school or college, how many hours did you spend to obtain a passing grade in a course in history or geography? And why did you enroll in that course? Is your everlasting destiny less worthy or consequential than a course in history or geography?

Examine the brief descriptions offered in the following section about several selected books and then decide which ones you wish to read. If "the demands of making a living" allow you to take only a few minutes a day for your spiritual life, then start with books that will help you pass swiftly through the three steps involved in the "***stage of seeing***:"

- ***Knowing Bahá'u'lláh***

- ***Examining His sacred Scriptures***

- ***Studying the prophecies He has fulfilled***

To gain an adequate knowledge about the preceding topics, you must engage in a serious study of the Bahá'í Faith. To accomplish this goal, consider reading the following books:

1. ***Bahá'u'lláh***: *The One Promised in all Scriptures*, 235 pages. To know a religion, it is essential to know its Founder—the One who planted the Tree of Life. Reading this book is a "must" for anyone who wishes to gain a deep knowledge of the Bahá'í Faith.

2. ***The Evidence for Bahá'u'lláh***: *The Glory of the Father*, 329 pages. This book presents 57 marks of distinction in the lives and teachings of Christ and Bahá'u'lláh to show that these two great Figures are identical, that they manifest the same marks of distinction. It offers many selections from their sacred Scriptures, as well as a summary of the hundreds of Biblical prophecies that Bahá'u'lláh has fulfilled. This book is especially written for Christians.

3. ***The Greatest News***: *The News Everyone Should Hear*, 166 pages. This book presents the roots of the Tree of Life. It is addressed to Christians to prove that the promise of the Second Advent has already been fulfilled.

4. ***Death: The Door to Heaven***, 182 pages. This book offers a spiritual perspective on this life and the life beyond.

5. ***God's 19 Great Little Tranquilizers***: *A Prescription for Peaceful and Purposeful Living*, 62 pages. This small book presents a summary of the spiritual principles and laws that are essential to a life of peace and happiness. It describes the transforming and healing powers gained from an intimate relationship with God. It is especially

helpful to agnostics and atheists, and to those who wish to become more spiritual without joining any religion.

6. ***Bahá'í Prayers***: *Prayer: the Key to the Heart of Heaven*, 226 pages. We are asked to recognize a tree by its fruits (Matt. 7:20). Prayers are the first fruits of religion—its heart and soul. They are the heavenly lights that guide us to the presence of God and manifest His glory and grandeur. The prayers offered in this book are a basketful of fruits from the Vineyard of ***Bahá'u'lláh—the Glory of God***. They have the power to inspire, to elevate and unite the followers of all religions. They serve as the center of unity and peace for all nations.

*He Whose advent hath been foretold in the heavenly Scriptures is come, could ye but understand it. The world's horizon is illumined by the splendors of this Most Great Revelation. Haste ye with radiant hearts and be not of them that are bereft of understanding.[6]*     *Bahá'u'lláh*

*"Come!" say the Spirit and the bride. "Come!" let each hearer reply. Come forward, you who are thirsty; accept the water of life, a free gift to all who desire it.*     *Christ (Rev. 22:17 NEB)*

*The Best-Beloved is come...All the favors of God have been sent down, as a token of His grace. The waters of everlasting life have, in their fullness, been proffered unto men. Every*

**single cup hath been borne round by the hand
of the Well-Beloved. Draw near, and tarry not,
though it be for one short moment.**[7]

**Bahá'u'lláh**

# Part V

## Prayers from Bahá'u'lláh

To recognize Him and follow Him, Jesus did not ask us to engage in debates! He asked us to pray:

> Take heed, watch and pray; for you do not know when the time is.
>
> Christ (Mark 13:33 NKJ)

> …pray always, that ye may be accounted worthy to escape all these things that shall come to pass, and to stand before the Son of man.
>
> Christ (Luke 21:36)

Why should we pray for receiving the honor of recognizing our Redeemer? Because without His permission and His blessings, we will be unable to know Him:

> No one can come to Me unless the Father who sent Me draws him…
>
> Christ (John 6:44 NKJ)

To help us attain the purpose for which we came into being and to become worthy of knowing Him, Bahá'u'lláh has revealed hundreds of prayers. The following are a few brief selections from a large volume: *Prayers and Meditations by Bahá'u'lláh.*

Unto Thee be praise, O Lord my God! I entreat Thee, by Thy signs that have encompassed the entire creation…to rend asunder the veils that shut me out from Thee, that I may… be immersed beneath the ocean of Thy nearness and pleasure.[1]

Suffer me not, O my Lord, to be deprived of the knowledge of Thee in Thy days, and divest me not of the robe of Thy guidance. Give me to drink of the river that is life indeed…that mine eyes may be opened, and my face be illumined, and my heart be assured, and my soul be enlightened, and my steps be made firm.[2]

Magnified be Thy name, O Lord my God! Thou art He Whom all things worship and Who worshipeth no one…I implore Thee…to enable me to drink deep of the living waters through which Thou hast vivified the hearts of Thy chosen ones and quickened the souls of them that love Thee, that I may, at all times and under all conditions, turn my face wholly towards Thee.

Thou art the God of power, of glory and bounty. No God is there beside Thee, the Supreme Ruler, the All-Glorious, the Omniscient.[3]

I beseech Thee, O my Lord…to rend asunder the veils that have hindered me from appearing before the throne of Thy majesty, and from standing at the door of Thy gate. Do Thou ordain for me, O my Lord, every good thing Thou didst send down in Thy Book, and suffer me not to be far removed from the shelter of Thy mercy.

Powerful art Thou to do what pleaseth Thee. Thou art, verily, the All-Powerful, the Most Generous.[4]

I beseech Thee, O Thou Who art my Companion in my lowliness, to rain down upon Thy loved ones from the clouds of Thy mercy that which will cause them to be satisfied with Thy pleasure, and will enable them to turn unto Thee and to be detached from all else except Thee. Ordain, then, for them every good conceived by Thee and predestined in Thy Book. Thou art, verily, the All-Powerful, He Whom nothing whatsoever can frustrate.[5]

Since Thou hast revealed Thy grace, O my God, deter not Thy servants from directing their eyes towards it. Consider not, O my God, their estate, and their concerns and their works. Consider the greatness of Thy glory, and the plenteousness of Thy gifts, and the power of Thy might, and the excellence of Thy favors. I swear by Thy glory! Wert Thou to look upon them with the eye of justice, all would deserve Thy wrath and the rod of Thine anger. Hold Thou Thy creatures, O my God, with the hands of Thy grace, and make Thou known unto them what is best for them of all the things that have been created in the kingdom of Thine invention.[6]

Blessed is he that hath set himself towards Thee…Blessed is he who with all his affections hath turned to the Dawning-Place of Thy Revelation and the Fountain-Head of Thine inspiration. Blessed is he that hath expended in Thy path what Thou didst bestow upon him through Thy bounty and favor. Blessed is he who, in his sore longing after Thee, hath cast away all else except Thyself. Blessed is he who hath enjoyed intimate communion with Thee, and rid himself of all attachment to any one save Thee.[7]

Lauded be Thy name, O my God! I entreat Thee…to blot out from my heart all idle fancies and vain imaginings, that with all my affections I may turn unto Thee, O Thou Lord of all mankind!

I am Thy servant…O my God! I have laid hold on the handle of Thy grace, and clung to the cord of Thy tender mercy. Ordain for me the good things that are with Thee, and nourish me from the Table Thou didst send down out of the clouds of Thy bounty and the heaven of Thy favor.

Thou, in very truth, art the Lord of the worlds, and the God of all that are in heaven and all that are on earth.[8]

Happy is the man who hath recognized Thee, and discovered the sweetness of Thy fragrance, and set himself towards Thy kingdom…Great is the blessedness of him who hath acknowledged Thy most excellent majesty, and whom the veils that have shut out the nations from Thee have not hindered from directing his eyes towards Thee, O Thou Who art the King of eternity…Blessed, moreover, be the man that hath turned unto Thee, and woe betide him that hath turned his back upon Thee.

Praised be Thou, the Lord of the worlds![9]

Glory be to Thee, O King of eternity…I pray Thee…to number me with such as have rid themselves from everything except Thyself, and have set themselves towards Thee…[10]

I have laid hold, O my Lord, on the handle of Thy bounty, and clung steadfastly to the hem of the robe of Thy favor. Send down, then, upon me, out of the clouds of Thy generosity, what will purge out from me the remembrance of any one except Thee, and make me able to turn unto Him Who is the Object of the adoration of all mankind…[11]

Suffer me, O my God, to draw nigh unto Thee, and to abide within the precincts of Thy court, for remoteness from Thee hath well-nigh consumed me. Cause me to rest under the shadow of the wings of Thy grace, for the flame of my separation from Thee hath melted my heart within me. Draw me nearer unto the river that is life indeed, for my soul burneth with thirst in its ceaseless search after Thee. My sighs, O my God, proclaim the bitterness of mine anguish, and the tears I shed attest my love for Thee.[12]

I beseech Thee…to grant that we may be numbered among them that have recognized Thee and acknowledged Thy sovereignty in Thy days. Help us then to quaff, O my God, from the fingers of mercy the living waters of Thy loving-kindness, that we may utterly forget all else except Thee, and be occupied only with Thy Self. Powerful art Thou to do what Thou willest. No God is there beside Thee, the Mighty, the Help in Peril, the Self-Subsisting.

Glorified be Thy name, O Thou Who art the King of all Kings![13]

Cast me not out, I implore Thee, of the presence of Thy grace, neither do Thou withhold from me the outpourings of Thy generosity and bounty. Ordain for me, O my Lord, what Thou hast ordained for them that love Thee, and write down for me what Thou hast written down for Thy chosen ones. My gaze hath, at all times, been fixed on the horizon of Thy gracious providence, and mine eyes bent upon the court of Thy tender mercies. Do with me as beseemeth Thee. No God is there but Thee, the God of power, the God of glory, Whose help is implored by all men.[14]

Deny me not, O my Lord, what is with Thee, and suffer me not to be forgetful of what Thou didst desire in Thy days. Thou art, verily, the Almighty, the Most Exalted, the All-Glorious, the All-Wise.[15]

Hold Thou the hand of this seeker who hath set his face towards Thee, O my Lord, and draw him out of the depths of his vain imaginations, that the light of certainty may shine brightly above the horizon of his heart…[16]

Praise be to Thee, O Lord my God!…I beseech Thee, by Him Who is the Fountain-Head of Thy Revelation and the Day-Spring of Thy signs, to make my heart to be a receptacle of Thy love and of remembrance of Thee. Knit it, then, to Thy most great Ocean, that from it may flow out the living waters of Thy wisdom and the crystal streams of Thy glorification and praise.[17]

I beg of Thee, O my God, by Thy most exalted Word…to ordain that my choice be conformed to Thy choice and my wish to Thy wish, that I may be entirely content with that which Thou didst desire, and be wholly satisfied with what Thou didst destine for me by Thy bounteousness and favor. Potent art Thou to do as Thou willest. Thou, in very truth, art the All-Glorious, the All-Wise.[18]

I implore Thee, by Thy name which Thou hast raised up above every other name, and hast caused to overshadow all that are in heaven and all that are on earth, to cast not away him that hath turned towards Thee, and to deny him not the wonders of Thy grace and the hidden evidences of Thy mercy. Let the hands of Thine omnipotence kindle in his heart a lamp that will enable him to shine brightly in Thy days...that Thou mayest behold him sanctified as Thou wishest and as beseemeth Thy majesty and glory.[19]

Lauded be Thy name, O my God and the God of all things, my Glory and the Glory of all things, my Desire and the Desire of all things, my Strength and the Strength of all things, my King and the King of all things, my Possessor and the Possessor of all things, my Aim and the Aim of all things, my Mover and the Mover of all things! Suffer me not, I implore Thee, to be kept back from the ocean of Thy tender mercies, nor to be far removed from the shores of nearness to Thee.[20]

O God!...the remembrance of Thee is a healing medicine to the hearts of such as have drawn nigh unto Thy court; nearness to Thee is the true life of them who are Thy lovers; Thy presence is the ardent desire of such as yearn to behold Thy face; remoteness from Thee is a torment to those that have acknowledged Thy oneness, and separation from Thee is death unto them that have recognized Thy truth![21]

Glory be to Thee, O my God! Thou hearest Thine ardent lovers lamenting in their separation from Thee...Open Thou outwardly to their faces, O my Lord, the gates of Thy grace, that they may enter them by Thy leave and in conformity with Thy will, and may stand before the throne of Thy majesty, and catch the accents of Thy voice, and be illumined with the splendors of the light of Thy face.

Potent art Thou to do what pleaseth Thee. None can withstand the power of Thy sovereign might.[22]

Have mercy, then, upon Thy servants by Thy grace and bounty, and suffer them not to be kept back from the shores of the ocean of Thy nearness. If Thou abandonest them, who is there to befriend them; and if Thou puttest them far from Thee, who is he that can favor them? They have none other Lord beside Thee, none to adore except Thyself. Deal Thou generously with them by Thy bountiful grace.

Thou, in truth, art the Ever-Forgiving, the Most Compassionate.[23]

I pray Thee, O Thou Who causest the dawn to appear...that Thou wilt grant that we may draw near unto what Thou didst destine for us by Thy favor and bounty, and to be far removed from whatsoever may be repugnant unto Thee. Give us, then, to drink from the hands of Thy grace every day and every moment of our lives of the waters that are life indeed, O Thou Who art the Most Merciful![24]

I am he who is sore athirst, O my Lord! Give me to drink of the living waters of Thy grace. I am but a poor creature; reveal unto me the tokens of Thy riches...

I beseech Thee, O my Lord, by Thy mercy that hath surpassed the entire creation, and Thy generosity that hath embraced all created things, to cause me to turn my face wholly towards Thee, and to seek Thy shelter, and to be steadfast in my love for Thee. Write down, then, for me what Thou didst ordain for them who love Thee.

Powerful art Thou to do what Thou pleasest. No God is there beside Thee, the Ever-Forgiving, the All-Bountiful.

Praised be God, the Lord of the worlds![25]

I testify, O my God, that this is the Day whereon Thy testimony hath been fulfilled, and Thy clear tokens have been manifested, and Thine utterances have been revealed, and Thy signs have been demonstrated, and the radiance of Thy countenance hath been diffused, and Thy proof hath been perfected, and Thine ascendancy hath been established, and Thy mercy hath overflowed, and the Day-Star of Thy grace hath shone forth with such brilliance that Thou didst manifest Him Who is the Revealer of Thyself and the Treasury of Thy wisdom and the Dawning-Place of Thy majesty and power.[26]

# Part VI

# Books that Can
# Change Your Destiny

- *Bahá'í Scriptures
  Available in English*

- *Books on the Bahá'í
  Faith by the Same
  Author*

# Bahá'í Scriptures
# Available in English

# Bahá'u'lláh's Works

Seek ye out the book of Jehovah and read...
*Isaiah 34:16*

## *Gleanings from the Writings of Bahá'u'lláh*

The most complete and comprehensive reference on Bahá'u'lláh's Works available in English. This book, which is a compilation from the Writings of Bahá'u'lláh, covers a wide spectrum of precepts ranging from the purpose of man's creation, his duty and destiny, to the manifold mysteries of divine Wisdom.

## *Prayers and Meditations By Bahá'u'lláh*

Bahá'u'lláh has left a rich repository of prayers pertaining to every human hope and aspiration, dream or desire. Thus, in this dispensation, the seekers of serenity, guidance, and inspiration can select and recite prayers and meditations revealed and blessed by the Pen of the Redeemer of the age, the revealer of divine Purpose.

Bahá'u'lláh has also written many prayers expressing His own supplication and servitude before God. Such prayers offer an intimate knowledge of Bahá'u'lláh's own self—His indomitable spirit, His unswerving love for the Creator and for humanity, His steadfastness in His claim, His determination before the onrush of adversities, His absolute trust in God, and His loving counsel to all those athirst for truth.

## *The Hidden Words of Bahá'u'lláh*

No other of Bahá'u'lláh's works so succinctly offers the reader as complete and as representative a sample of the ethical fruits of the new Revelation as *The Hidden Words*. It is a small book filled with gems, a treasure-house of celestial Wisdom, a divine guide to the unfoldment and ennoblement of the human spirit.

All the requirements for attaining purity and self-fulfillment are stated in the most exquisite and lofty language. Everything that the soul must seek or surrender, everything that a spiritual seeker must know or must do to direct the course of his or her spiritual destiny is concisely and clearly revealed and set forth by the pen of the Supreme Messenger—the Revealer of hidden wisdom and divine mysteries.

## The Seven Valleys and the Four Valleys

Perhaps the most mystical of Bahá'u'lláh's works available in English. It unfolds and enumerates the stages of seeker's journey towards God; revealing, in a language at once poetic and perplexing, his potential for attaining perfection and nobility, and his sublime and celestial destiny, if he but turns to the light instead of darkness, seeks the gems of divine wisdom instead of the perishable joys of flesh, and undertakes to tread the long but wondrous and enchanting path of purification and illumination.

## Epistle to the Son of the Wolf

Addressed to a cruel and cunning Muslim clergyman who, along with his father, inflicted death, distress, and torment on some of Bahá'u'lláh's most beloved and most distinguished disciples. Though addressed to a symbol of denial, it is a call to humanity as a whole. This weighty volume covers and clarifies many illuminating and inspiring arrays of precepts.

## The Summons of the Lord of Hosts

Contains some of Bahá'u'lláh's Epistles or Tablets addressed to the kings and rulers of the world, to its religious leaders, and to humanity in general. These Tablets comprise Bahá'u'lláh's most emphatic words on His claim and on His station as the supreme Savior of humankind, the King of Kings, the Glory of the Lord, the Desire of the Nations, the Everlasting Father, the Prince of Peace, the Lord of the Vineyard, Christ returned in the Glory of the Father, the Inaugurator of the Cycle of Fulfillment, and the Promised One of all ages and religions.

## *The Book of Certitude*✧

This book responds to questions raised by a seeker of truth. It unseals "the sealed Wine of mysteries," and unveils the symbolism and the essence of all the scriptures of the past, indicates how the seeker of truth can rise above the prevailing perplexity and confusion, how he or she can move from doubt to certitude, and from unbelief to belief.

It offers proofs of divine Revelation, portrays in a moving language man's refusal to accept and acknowledge, in every age, the gift of divine Guidance, and conveys in a unique tone and style the dramatic story of the unfoldment of the perennial Faith of God, the unveiling of the eternal Truth.

---

✧Also known as *The Kitáb-i-Íqán.*

## Other Bahá'í Writings
## Available in English

### By Bahá'u'lláh:

*The Most Holy Book*
*Tablets of Bahá'u'lláh*
*Gems of Divine Mysteries*
*Tabernacle of Unity*

---

### By the Báb:

*Selections from the Writings of the Báb*

---

### By 'Abdu'l-Bahá:

*Some Answered Questions*
*Foundations of World Unity*
*The Secret of Divine Civilization*
*Paris Talks*
*Selections from the Writings of 'Abdu'l-Bahá*
*The Promulgation of Universal Peace*
*A Traveller's Narrative*

# Books on the Bahá'í Faith by the Same Author

- Evidence for the Bahá'í Faith
- History and Teachings
- The Afterlife
- Forthcoming Books

# Evidence for
# the Bahá'í Faith

*I Shall Come Again*
522 Pages
Volume I

*That is the day when I come like a thief.
Happy the man who stays awake.*
*Christ (Rev. 16:15)*

*Do not let Him find you sleeping. What I
say to you, I say to everyone: "Watch!"*
*Christ (Mark 13:36)*

Did you know that the Bible contains 16 time
prophecies concerning the year of the Second Advent? No wonder so many scholars discovered the
same date. Did you also know that all those 16
prophecies point to the same year: 1844? ***Bahá'ís
believe that the promise of the Second Advent has***

**already been fulfilled, precisely as predicted.** Christ did return in 1844, "**like a thief**," in a way that **the News of His coming did not draw much attention**. And as the Book of Revelation predicts, God gave Him a new name: **Bahá'u'lláh**, meaning **the Glory of God**.

Obviously **we expect you to be very skeptical**, but we invite you **to stay spiritually awake, to "watch," to pay close attention, and to investigate this most glorious News**. How can you do this? Start your search by examining the evidence presented in **I Shall Come Again**, the first of a six-volume series on the fulfillment of biblical prophecies by **Bahá'u'lláh, the Glory of God**.

**I Shall Come Again**, written after three decades of research, takes you step by step through 16 prophecies that point to 1844, and hundreds of other prophecies, concerning the return of Christ. It proves how these prophecies, without exception, were fulfilled by **Bahá'u'lláh (the Glory of God)** and His martyred Herald, **the Báb (the Gate)**, who appeared in 1844. **I Shall Come Again** is one of the most fascinating books of our time. If you have faith in God's promises and a desire to know the truth, you will receive incomparable joy and hope from reading it.

History shows that no false prophet has ever been able to prove his claim by the evidence of fulfilled prophecies. Christian scholars often regard Hebrew prophecies as the most conclusive and convincing evidence of Jesus' divine Mission.

Let us consider a statement from Dr. Norman Geisler, president of Southern Evangelical Seminary, "who has published countless articles in academic journals and has authored over fifty books, including *Baker Encyclopedia of Christian Apologetics*." Dr. Geisler makes the following statement concerning the prophecies that point to the First Advent of Jesus:

> Some have suggested...that the prophecies were accidentally fulfilled in Jesus. In other words, he happened to be in the right place at the right time...If there is a God who is in control of the universe, as we have said, then chance is ruled out. Furthermore, it is unlikely that these events would have converged in the life of one man. Mathematicians have calculated the probability of 16 predictions being fulfilled in one man at 1 in $10^{45}$...

> But it is not just a logical improbability that rules out this theory [of chance]; it is the moral implausibility of an all-powerful and all-knowing God letting things get out of control so that all his plans for prophetic fulfillment are ruined by someone who just happened to be in the right place at the right time. God cannot lie, nor can he break a promise (Heb. 6:18). So we must conclude that he did not allow his prophetic promises to be thwarted by chance. All the evidence points to Jesus as the divinely appointed fulfillment of the Messianic prophecies. He was God's man confirmed by God's signs. In brief, if God made the predictions to be fulfilled in the

life of Christ, then he would not allow them to be fulfilled in the life of any other. The God of truth would not allow a lie to be confirmed as true.

*Imagine if the News of the Return of Jesus is true and you choose not to investigate and not to know Him! Imagine also if the News of His Return is true and your investigation leads you to recognize Him!*

*I shall come again and receive you to myself, so that where I am you may be also.*
*Christ (John 14:3)*

*"He, verily, is come with His Kingdom, and all the atoms cry aloud: 'Lo! The Lord is come in His great majesty!'" "Behold how He hath come down from the heaven of His grace, girded with power and invested with sovereignty. Is there any doubt concerning His signs?"*
*Bahá'u'lláh (the Glory of God)*

### Lord of Lords
634 Pages
Volume II

This volume presents hundreds of biblical prophecies concerning the Central Figures of the Bahá'í Faith—the Báb, Bahá'u'lláh, 'Abdu'l-Bahá—as well as Shoghi Effendi (the Guardian of the Bahá'í

Faith), the Universal House of Justice (the supreme administrative body in the Bahá'í Faith), the Bahá'ís (the followers of Bahá'u'lláh), the Bahá'í teachings, and the Book of Bahá'í Laws (*The Kitáb-i-Aqdas*).

*Lord of Lords* presents six fulfillments for Daniel's prophecy of 1335, and shows their connection to the Bahá'í Faith. The book also presents *86 similarities between Jesus and the Báb*, who is called *"One like a Son of Man."*

Christian scholars often apply the statistical laws to the prophecies of Hebrew Scriptures to prove the divine station of Jesus. *Lord of Lords* applies the same laws to the prophecies of both Hebrew and Christian Scriptures to prove the divine station of the Báb and Bahá'u'lláh.

*Lord of Lords* shows that the probability of biblical prophecies coming true in the Bahá'í Faith by chance alone is about 1 in $10^{80}$. The number $10^{80}$ is equal to the number of atoms in the known universe! What does this evidence indicate? *It indicates that if anyone could pick a specific atom in the universe by chance, he could then claim that the biblical prophecies fulfilled in the Bahá'í Faith also happened by chance!* The proof presented in this volume is so compelling it can convince even the most skeptic seeker!

> *...the desire of all nations shall come...*
> *Haggai 2:7*

> *He who is the Desired One is come in His transcendent majesty...Better is this for you than all ye possess.* *Bahá'u'lláh (the Glory of God)*

*For the Son of man shall come in the glory of his Father...*          Christ (Matt. 16:27)

*I have come in the shadows of the clouds of glory, and am invested by God with invincible sovereignty.*          Bahá'u'lláh (the Glory of God)

***King of Kings***
510 Pages
Volume III

This is the third of the six-volume series. This volume also presents hundreds of biblical prophecies concerning the advent of the Bahá'í Faith. Four of its chapters show that, contrary to what most people —both Christians and Jews—believe, *the Bible predicts suffering and severe persecution for the Redeemer of our time. King of Kings* also presents many prophecies, in the course of two chapters, to show that according to both Testaments, the title of the Redeemer of our age (known to Christians as the Second Coming of Christ and to the Jews as the Messiah) is "*the Glory of God,*" the English translation of the original title "*Bahá'u'lláh.*"

A chapter discusses the many reasons why people deny and persecute their promised Messenger and Redeemer in every age, and then later claim that if they had lived at the time of His Advent they would not be among the deniers!

Many Christians expect the coming of the Anti-christ. ***King of Kings*** presents two chapters to show the fulfillment of this expectation by two deceptive figures who opposed ***Bahá'u'lláh, the Glory of God***, with all their might, and tried in vain to destroy Him and establish themselves as the Central Figures of the Bahá'í Faith.

***I Shall Come Again***, ***Lord of Lords***, and ***King of Kings*** prove that once again God has spoken to humanity, that He has fulfilled His promises, and has manifested His great glory and power by send-ing two supreme Messengers and Redeemers—***Bahá'u'lláh, and His martyred Herald, the Báb***—to guide our bewildered world to unity, peace, and justice, and to lead our wandering souls to His heavenly Mansions. Not investigating this Message of hope and fulfillment is to deprive yourself of the very source of all wisdom and the very purpose of coming to this world.

> *I have come down from heaven...*
> *Christ (John 6:38)*

> *Say, God is my witness! The Promised One Himself [Bahá'u'lláh] hath come down from heaven...with the hosts of revelation on His right, and the angels of inspiration on His left...* *Bahá'u'lláh (the Glory of God)*

> *Behold, I come like a thief! Blessed is he who stays awake...* *Christ (Rev. 16:15)*

> *Blessed the slumberer who is awakened... Blessed the ear that hath heard, and the eye*

*that hath seen, and the heart that hath turned unto Him...*        *Bahá'u'lláh (the Glory of God)*

# What do others say about:

I Shall Come Again, Lord of Lords,
King of Kings?

*A scholarly work of meticulous research. Appealing to reason and applying the scientific method to prophetic scripture, it demonstrates that God has once again revealed Himself to humankind and has provided hope for unity and peace on this planet.* **John Paul Vader, M.D.**
Author of *For the Good of Mankind*

*A book with a message of hope and fulfillment, a message that can transform our planet into a place of peace, into a kingdom that has been the dream and hope of humanity since the dawn of history...a scholarly, comprehensive, and fascinating work that has been long overdue. No wonder it took over three decades to complete it.* **Hon. Dorothy W. Nelson**
Judge, U. S. Court of Appeals, 9th Circuit

*A story with an incredible ending that is made credible by the sheer weight of evidence. It is a must for anyone interested in the proofs of the advent of the Promised One of all ages.*

**John Huddleston**
Former Chief of Budget and Planning
Division, International Monetary Fund,
Author of *The Earth Is But One Country*

*...a treasure house of great value for both Bahá'ís and seekers.* **Adib Taherzadeh**
Author and Scholar

*I am in awe at the extent of research you have undertaken!* **Waldo Boyd**
Writer and Editor

*Your work never fails to astound me. The effort and breadth of your knowledge both of the Bible and other literature as well as the depth of your understanding of Bahá'í Scripture is truly amazing. Also, a hallmark of your work is your thoroughness. Anyone who believes in biblical prophecy, and reads these volumes with an open mind, cannot fail to be convinced.*
**Dr. Tom Rowe**
Professor of Psychology

*Your work is the best I've seen on biblical prophecies and proofs of Bahá'u'lláh's Revelation. You offer so much information in relatively few pages. Your many references prove clearly the book's central claim. Your language is simple and exciting. You take the reader through a complete spiritual and prophetic adventure. Your approach is modest, yet dynamic. I pray it will excite all your readers as it has excited me.* **Joe Killeen**
Bible Scholar, with a Degree in
Eschatology and Soteriology

*There are few works by a single author that can rival Dr. Motlagh's in their sheer scope, depth and thoroughness of scholarship. Without doubt, future Bahá'ís will thank Dr. Motlagh for his achievements, that are, in my opinion, not only astonishing—they are heroic.*

*An important work that will be referenced by future Bahá'í scholars for millennia to come.*

**Robert F. Riggs**
Aerospace and Marine Scientist, Inventor,
Author of *The Apocalypse Unsealed*

*By writing these volumes Dr. Motlagh has made a momentous contribution to our understanding of biblical prophecy. As a former Baptist minister, I urge all Christians to investigate the news of the return of our Lord as presented in* **I Shall Come Again, Lord of Lords,** *and* **King of Kings.** *"Arise, shine, for your light has come, and the glory of the Lord rises upon you" (Isa. 60:1).*

**Mel Campbell**
Former Baptist Minister

## Come Now, Let Us Reason Together

286 Pages

This book is written in response to the objections raised by a pastor against the Bahá'í Faith. *It removes all the main obstacles that prevent Christians from recognizing the return of the Son in the glory of the Father*, from acknowledging the promised

Redeemer of our time—***Bahá'u'lláh, the Glory of God***. Once you start reading this book, you will find it hard to put down.

### *The Evidence for Bahá'u'lláh*:
**The Glory of the Father**
329 pages

One way to prove that Bahá'u'lláh fulfills the promise of the Second Advent is to compare Him with Jesus Christ. ***The Evidence for Bahá'u'lláh***: *The Glory of the Father*, does exactly that. It compares Jesus and Bahá'u'lláh in 35 different ways. A fair-minded, even a skeptical, reader cannot escape this conclusion: If Jesus is the One He claims to be, so must be Bahá'u'lláh. A sincere Christian cannot in good faith accept One and reject the other. It will be like having twin children, but loving only one of them!

In addition, ***The Evidence for Bahá'u'lláh*** offers a summary of some of the most significant prophecies presented in ***I Shall Come Again***, ***Lord of Lords***, and ***King of Kings***.

# History and Teachings

***On Wings of
Destiny***

274 Pages

***On Wings of Destiny*** is based on a dialogue between two friends. Reading it is like joining a circle
of friends and participating in a "fireside chat."

The prime purpose of the book is to inspire you—
and anyone else who values his soul and spiritual
life—to recognize that *in this world you have an
awesome responsibility: you must choose your
everlasting destiny. That choice has unimaginable
consequences that will endure beyond death for
all eternity*. Failing to make a choice is also a
choice. This book invites you to make every effort
to discover God's plan for you and to follow that
plan.

***On Wings of Destiny*** shows that the only way you
can attain true joy and happiness in all the worlds
of God is to cultivate your spiritual potential and
to draw nearer and nearer to God. If you value your
soul and wish to choose your destiny in the light
of knowledge and freedom, take the time to listen
to this inspiring "fireside chat" to discover how the
Bahá'í teachings can help you attain contentment,

fulfill your life's purpose, and discover your divine destiny: Heaven's most glorious gift to you.

### *Choosing Your Destiny*
375 Pages

Most people leave their destiny to "chance." Whatever their parents happen to believe, they believe. This book shows that our "destiny" is God's most precious gift to us. Should we throw this gift to the wind? Should we allow "chance" rather than "choice" determine our destiny?

The Bahá'í Faith has come to give us spiritual insight and to help us choose our destiny in the light of reason and true knowledge, rather than in the darkness of tradition and conformity. The knowledge contained in *Choosing Your Destiny* can liberate us from past prejudices and illusions and set our souls free. It can help us become spiritual by developing "the divine image" in our soul.

### *One God, Many Faiths; One Garden, Many Flowers*
290 Pages

***One God, Many Faiths; One Garden, Many Flowers*** shows that in God's garden there are many fragrant flowers, planted and nourished by the same Gardener. The Bahá'í Faith has come to help us recognize the beauty of the garden, the harmony of the flowers, and the oneness of the Gardener.

When we realize that we are all one people, on one planet, under one God, with one common destiny, the walls of prejudice that divide God's beautiful garden will crumble. Only true knowledge and love can reveal this beauty and bring about this wonder. The Bahá'í Faith is that knowledge and that love. It penetrates the hearts and souls of humankind to dispel all shadows of prejudice and separation. It connects our hearts and reveals the beauty and splendor of our souls in the light of oneness. ***One God, Many Faiths, One Garden, Many Flowers*** offers you the knowledge that can change your destiny.

# The Afterlife

### *Unto God Shall We Return*
164 pages

This is a compilation from the Bahá'í Scriptures on the afterlife. It brings together the Writings of Bahá'u'lláh, the Báb, and 'Abdu'l-Bahá on the purpose of human life and the continuation of that purpose into the mysterious realms beyond. *Unto God Shall We Return* is compiled and arranged to portray a clear vision of the meaning of life—both here and hereafter—and to offer guidance about how we can prepare our soul for God's "many mansions in heaven."

### *The Glorious Journey to God*
256 Pages

*The Glorious Journey to God* contains quotations from the Bible, the Qur'án, and Bahá'í Scriptures on the Afterlife. The book shows a remarkable similarity between these sacred Scriptures.

## *A Messenger of Joy*
### 112 Pages

*A Messenger of Joy* is the most comforting and positive book ever written on death and the afterlife. In consoling and uplifting the souls of the grieving, it sets a standard that is not likely to be surpassed for a long time.

This book portrays death as a message of joy and hope, and not as the news of sorrow and despair. It lifts the veil to show that death is not the end of life, but the beginning of an everlasting and most glorious journey toward God.

## *A Glimpse of Paradise*
### A Near-Death Vision of the Next Life

This DVD (also video) contains a talk given by Reinee Pasarow about one of her near death visions. This is a state in which the individual shows no vital signs of life, yet experiences life to its fullest. What makes this story unique is this: Reinee's vision guided her to become a Bahá'í. She was given several clues by a spiritual being about the Bahá'í Faith. For instance, one of the titles of Bahá'u'lláh—

the Blessed Beauty—was revealed to her. She was also told the word "justice" and shown the seat of the Universal House of Justice, exactly as it is built. Reinee had many unusual dreams as a child, and three near death visions.

We have added an introduction and a conclusion to this DVD to make it more attractive and meaningful to all viewers, especially to seekers. The introduction and conclusion present Biblical and Bahá'í references to the many clues that Mrs. Pasarow received while in the presence of the Being of Light.

# Knowing and Loving God

## *God's 19 Great Little Tranquilizers*
62 Pages

This is God's prescription for peaceful living. Without knowing, accepting, and living by these principles, no one can attain true happiness. This mini-book presents briefly the 19 most significant spiritual principles that bind us to our Creator.

# Forthcoming Books

## *The Evidence for Jesus*
### The Glory of the Son

It is absolutely essential to know why we believe in Jesus. Where can we find the answer? Only in the Words of Jesus Himself. *The Evidence for Jesus* offers a brief summary of all the reasons Jesus—not His followers—gave to substantiate His claim. This is a book that every Christian should read. It will also be of great value to those of the Jewish faith who have a desire to know the evidence for their glorious King and Redeemer: Jesus Christ.

## *Will Jesus Come from the Sky or as a Thief?*

*Be always on the watch!*  *Luke 21:36*

*The day of the Lord will come like a thief in the night.*  *I Thess. 5:2*

In the mid-19th century many Christian scholars had discovered that, according to numerous biblical prophecies and promises, Christ would return in 1844. Thousands of Christians around the world expected His Return in that year. Why did so many discover the same date? And what piece of "the prophetic puzzle" did they miss? Let us explore this critical question.

Jesus declared that He would return "***like a thief***." He also repeatedly warned us to "***Watch!***" How does a thief come? Secretly. A thief does not want to draw attention to himself. This is his foremost concern. How can we catch a thief? By being awake and "***watchful***," by "***paying attention***" to his coming. Jesus' warning that He would return "***like a thief***," and His recommended strategy for recognizing Him by staying ***awake*** and by "***watching***" for Him, are complementary:

### *The warning: I shall come like a thief!*

### *The way to recognize me: Watch, pay close attention! Do not be complacent!*

What, then, did Jesus mean by warning us repeatedly and emphatically to "***Watch!***"? He meant: "***Pay close attention to the news of My coming!***"

How did Jesus come the first time? Like a thief. He walked among the Jews. He knew every one of them, but with a few exceptions, they did not know Him. Jesus concealed His supreme glory from "the strangers," from all those who were unworthy of seeing the Spirit of God in Him (John 12:40), from all those who "***may look and look but see nothing***" (Mark 10:12). ***Only the spiritually-sighted paid close attention to Him***, only they "watched" with their hearts and souls, and only they saw the glory of God in Him. Jesus did not allow the spiritually blind to witness His divine glory.

By the vivid expression "*like a thief*" Jesus instructs us to expect a repetition of the way He came the first time. He further confirms this fact by predicting that ***people will respond to the News of His coming the same way that they responded to the News of the coming of Noah***. They will be complacent, non-attentive, negligent, and spiritually asleep!

What piece of "the prophetic puzzle" did Christians (who expected the Return of Christ in 1844) miss? The same "piece" that the Jews had missed 18 centuries earlier and are still missing! That piece is the word "***SPIRIT:***"

## *The "missing piece" for Jews:*

He will come as a "*king*" means: "*His Spirit* will come as a king."

## *The "missing piece" for Christians:*

He will come from ***heaven*** means: "***His Spirit*** will come from heaven."

Jesus Himself decoded the word "sky" or "heaven" several times. Compare the following two verses, one from ***Jesus Christ, the Anointed One of God***; the other from ***Bahá'u'lláh, the Glory of God***:

> *I [the Spirit of God, Christ] have come down from heaven.*          *Christ (John 6:38)*

*He [the Spirit of God, Bahá'u'lláh], verily, hath again come down from heaven, even as He came down from it the first time.*

*Bahá'u'lláh (the Glory of God)*

### *Muhammad: the Spirit Who Glorified Jesus*

This book introduces Islam from a Bahá'í perspective. It demonstrates a remarkable harmony between the Bible and the Qur'án. It also responds to the objections raised against Islam.

### *The Spiritual Design of Creation*

This book is written to refresh the life of the soul. Its prime purpose is to advance the "knowledge of God," so that we may know our Creator as He really is, not as we may wish Him to be!

A poet once said: "God is closer to me than I am to myself. Why, then, am I so far from Him?" How can this be possible? The distance between our spirit and the Spirit of God can be measured by the difference between God as He really is, and the God that we have created in our mind. The purpose of acquiring the "knowledge of God" is to diminish the distance. The more we know God as He really is, the closer we draw to Him.

Our purpose in coming to this world is spiritual transformation, which can be attained only by knowing and loving God. *The Spiritual Design of Creation* will help you attain this Most Glorious Purpose. It appeals both to the mind and to the heart. It satisfies the mind by presenting the latest scientific evidence for the existence of God and the afterlife. It inspires and transforms the heart by showing the everlasting honors and rewards in store for those who cultivate their spiritual potential and the unimaginable losses for those who fail in this endeavor.

How would you feel if you traveled for 70 years toward a destination, and then at the end of this journey, you suddenly discovered that you had traveled in the wrong direction? This is the way many people squander the precious days of their lives. Imagine their disappointment at the end of their spiritual journey! Should we not then learn a lesson from their lives? Should we not take a little time for our soul while we still have a chance?

# Appendix

# A Letter for New Seekers

The following is a copy of a letter that I give to many of those with whom I share the news of the Advent of Bahá'u'lláh. Please feel free to reproduce copies.

> O my God!...I am sore athirst; give me to drink of the oceans of Thy bountiful favor. I am a stranger; draw me nearer unto the source of Thy gifts. I am sick; sprinkle upon me the healing waters of Thy grace. I am a captive; rid me of my bondage, by the power of Thy might and through the force of Thy will, that I may soar on the wings of detachment towards the loftiest summits of Thy creation.[1]      Bahá'u'lláh

## Dear Friend:

You should feel honored to be among those who have heard the news of the Advent of Bahá'u'lláh, the Glory of God. I pray that your knowledge will lead you to His Presence. The first requirement for success is removing "the veils of idle fancies" or "unverified and false assumptions" that surround us:

> …free thyself from *the veils of idle fancies* and enter into My court, that thou mayest be fit for everlasting life and worthy to meet Me.[2]                    Bahá'u'lláh

Only by removing "the veils" can the light of knowledge reach us and lead us to *true faith.* Only then can we attain the honor of *seeing the glory of God.*

> Did I not tell you that if you have *faith*, you will *see the glory of God*?"
> Christ (John 11:40 NEB)

Prophecies declare that among the many who are "called" only *a few* will succeed in freeing their souls from "the veils." Only *a few* will be able to join the ranks of the ones chosen by God:

> ...*many* are called, but *few* chosen.
> Christ (Matt. 20:16 NKJ)

In this letter I wish to share with you some insight about the choices you will make. Over the years I have noticed that those who are called to know Bahá'u'lláh fall into one of these groups:

- Many of them fail to investigate His message beyond their first exposure.

- Some of them investigate His message for a while—perhaps for a few weeks or months—and then stop.

- A few of them continue their investigation until they arrive at a conclusion.

Do you belong to the first, the second, or the third group? You will soon discover for yourself. You have, of course, full freedom to join the ranks of any group that you wish. I hope and pray that you will choose to join the ranks of the third group by continuing your investigation. To help you make the best choice, let me remind you of a universal law found in all the sacred Scriptures. It is *the Law of Reciprocity*. According to this Law, God will treat us the way we treat Him:

*For with the same measure that you use, it will be measured back to you.*
*Christ (Luke 6:38 NKJ)*

Let us now apply *the Law of Reciprocity* to the consequence of accepting or rejecting God's invitation to investigate the news of the Advent of His great Messengers and Redeemers. Only God has the authority to set these laws, to speak in this language, and to give such warnings:

> But he who denies Me before men will be denied before the angels of God.
> Christ (Luke 12:9)

> God will verily do unto them that which they themselves are doing, and will forget them even as they have ignored His Presence in His day. Such is His decree unto those that have denied Him, and such will it be unto them that have rejected His signs.[3]    Bahá'u'lláh

Recognition of *the Law of Reciprocity* will empower our soul with "fear of God"—an awareness of His awesome authority—and then it will lead us to wisdom, the most precious of all virtues:

The fear of the Lord is the beginning of wisdom...    Psalms 111:10

The essence of wisdom is the fear of God...and the apprehension of His justice and decree.[4]    Bahá'u'lláh

Hearing about the News of the Advent of Bahá'u'lláh not only offers you a chance to attain the greatest glory and honor, it also places a special responsibility on your conscience. This is because after you hear the News, a second law takes effect. It is *the Law of Justice*, expressed in these words:

*From everyone who has been given much, much will be demanded*; and from the one who has been entrusted with much, much more will be asked.
    Christ (Luke 12:48 NIV)

This letter expresses my love for all those seekers with whom I share this Greatest and most Glorious News: the Advent of the Glory of God—the One for whom the world has been awaiting for thousands of years. Its purpose is to help you recognize the great honor of hearing about Bahá'u'lláh and the heavenly fruits that this knowledge can bear for you for all eternity. I hope and pray that you will make every effort to join the third group by responding positively—with all your heart and soul—to God's invitation to investigate the news of the Advent of His new Messenger and Redeemer, Bahá'u'lláh, the Glory of God.

My experience shows that almost all people are quite busy. If that is a good reason for ignoring this News, then where can we find those who will investigate this News? Should we look for them in outer space? Devoting even as little as ten minutes a day will allow you to join the third group. Even five minutes a day may keep the flame of your search alive, and would show your devotion to God and to what He has planned for you.

If your car starts one out of three times, do you consider it faithful?

If you fail to come to work two or three times a month, does your boss call you faithful?

If your water heater greets you with cold water once in a while, do you call it faithful?

If you miss a couple of mortgage payments a year, does the loan company say, "Oh, well, 10 out of 12 is not too bad"?

If we expect faithfulness from other people and things, does not God expect the same—if not more—from us?

If at this point in your life, even five minutes a day is too much for you to devote to your everlasting destiny, then you may wish to keep this letter as a reminder to do in the future what you cannot do now.

May God give you plenty of time to investigate the news of the Advent of Bahá'u'lláh—the most awesome revelation of Knowledge from God—before your share of time has come to an end. May God bless you and aid you in all your endeavors.

> Magnified be Thy name, O Lord my God! Thou art He Whom all things worship and Who worshipeth no one… I implore Thee…to enable me to drink deep of the living waters through which Thou hast vivified the hearts of Thy chosen ones and quickened the souls of them that love Thee, that I may, at all times and under all conditions, turn my face wholly towards Thee.

Thou art the God of power, of glory and bounty. No God is there beside Thee, the Supreme Ruler, the All-Glorious, the Omniscient.[5]     Bahá'u'lláh

*With loving greetings,*

*Hugh Motlagh*

# References

## *The Promise of All Ages*

1. *Tablets of Bahá'u'lláh*, p. 11.
2. *Some Answered Questions*, 1981 ed., p. 63.
3. *Gleanings from the Writings of Bahá'u'lláh*, p. 7.
4. *Gleanings from the Writings of Bahá'u'lláh*, p. 288.

## *Brief Answers to Questions About the Bahá'í Faith*

1. Dyer, Wayne. *You'll See It When You Believe It,* New York: Avon Books, 1989, p. 163.
2. Dyer, Wayne. *You'll See It When You Believe It,* New York: Avon Books, 1989, pp. 164-165.
3. *Prayers and Meditations by Bahá'u'lláh*, p. 314.
4. *Selections from the Writings of the Báb*, p. 217.
5. *Prayers and Meditations by Bahá'u'lláh*, p. 251.
6. *Welcome to the Bahá'í House of Worship,* p. 5.
7. *Welcome to the Bahá'í House of Worship,* p. 5.
8. Moody, Raymond A. *Life After Life*, New York: Bantam Books, 1975, p. i.
9. *Gleanings from the Writings of Bahá'u'lláh*, pp. 85-86.

10. *Tablets of Bahá'u'lláh,* p. 50.

11. *Gleanings from the Writings of Bahá'u'lláh*, p. 31.

12. *The Kitáb-i-Íqán*, p. 24.

13. *Gleanings from the Writings of Bahá'u'lláh*, p. 159.

## *Bahá'u'lláh the Glory of God*

1. *The Beloved of the World* (translated from Persian), p. 184.

2. *The Beloved of the World* (translated from Persian), p. 184.

3. Marks, Geoffry W. *Call to Remembrance*, Wilmette, IL: Bahá'í Publishing Trust, 1992, p. 8.

4. Marks, Geoffry W. *Call to Remembrance*, Wilmette, IL: Bahá'í Publishing Trust, 1992, p. 11.

5. Marks, Geoffry W. *Call to Remembrance*, Wilmette, IL: Bahá'í Publishing Trust, 1992, p. 11.

6. *Teacher Training Manual for Children's Classes, Age 6*, Columbia: Ruhi Institute, 1992, Section 3, pp. 7-8.

7. Marks, Geoffry W. *Call to Remembrance*, Wilmette, IL: Bahá'í Publishing Trust, 1992, pp. 14-15.

8. *Paris Talks*, p. 76.

9. *Epistle to the Son of the Wolf*, p. 21.

10. *Gleanings from the Writings of Bahá'u'lláh*, p. 91.

11. *The Proclamation of Bahá'u'lláh*, p. 57.

12. *The Hidden Words of Bahá'u'lláh* (Persian), no. 52.

13. Marks, Geoffry W. *Call to Remembrance*, Wilmette, IL: Bahá'í Publishing Trust, 1992, pp. 166-167.

14. Momen, Wendi (ed.). *A Basic Bahá'í Dictionary*, Oxford: George Ronald, 1989, p. 155.

15. Momen, Wendi (ed.). *A Basic Bahá'í Dictionary*, Oxford: George Ronald, 1989, p. 155.

16. Marks, Geoffry W. *Call to Remembrance*, Wilmette, IL: Bahá'í Publishing Trust, 1992, pp. 169.

17. Quoted in *Bahá'u'lláh, A Brief Introduction to His Life and Work*, National Spiritual Assembly of the Bahá'ís of the United States, 1991, p. 31.

18. *Paris Talks*, p. 79.

19. *Some Answered Questions*, 1981 ed., p. 35.

## *Wake Up! I Shall Come Upon You Like a Thief!*

1. *Gleanings from the Writings of Bahá'u'lláh*, p. 319.

2. *Tablets of Bahá'u'lláh,* p. 258-259.

3. *Gleanings from the Writings of Bahá'u'lláh*, p. 45.

4. *Tablets of Bahá'u'lláh,* p. 244.

5. *Tablets of Bahá'u'lláh,* p. 75.

6. *Tablets of Bahá'u'lláh,* p. 41.

7. Shoghi Effendi. *The World Order of Bahá'u'lláh*, Wilmette, IL: Bahá'í Publishing Trust, 1980, p. 60.

8. *Tablets of Bahá'u'lláh,* pp. 78-79.

9. *Gleanings from the Writings of Bahá'u'lláh*, pp. 12-13.

10. *Tablets of Bahá'u'lláh*, pp. 9-10.

11. *Tablets of Bahá'u'lláh,* p. 10.

12. *Selections from the Writings of the Báb*, p. 134.

13. *Gleanings from the Writings of Bahá'u'lláh*, p. 144.

14. *The Proclamation of Bahá'u'lláh*, p. 121.

15. *Bahá'í Prayers*, Wilmette, IL: Bahá'í Publishing Trust, 1991 edition, p. 220.

16. *Selections from the Writings of the Báb*, p. 134.

17. *Selections from the Writings of the Báb*, p. 87.

18. *Gleanings from the Writings of Bahá'u'lláh*, p. 148.

19. Shoghi Effendi. *The Promised Day Is Come*, Wilmette, IL: Bahá'í publishing Committee, 1941, p. 5.

20. *Gleanings from the Writings of Bahá'u'lláh*, p. 17.

21. Shoghi Effendi. *The Promised Day Is Come*, Wilmette, IL: Bahá'í publishing Committee, 1941, p. 5.

22. *Gleanings from the Writings of Bahá'u'lláh*, p. 7.

23. *Gleanings from the Writings of Bahá'u'lláh*, p. 136.

24. *Gleanings from the Writings of Bahá'u'lláh*, p. 313.

25. Shoghi Effendi. *The World Order of Bahá'u'lláh*, Wilmette, IL: Bahá'í Publishing Trust, 1980, p. 107.

26. *Selections from the Writings of the Báb*, p. 161.

27. *Selections from the Writings of the Báb*, p. 61.

28. *Tablets of Bahá'u'lláh,* p. 242.

29. *The Hidden Words of Bahá'u'lláh* (Arabic), no. 63.

30. *Tablets of Bahá'u'lláh,* p. 41.

31. *Gleanings from the Writings of Bahá'u'lláh*, p. 325.

32. *Epistle to the Son of the Wolf*, p. 38.

## *Proofs of the Bahá'í Faith*

1. *Gleanings from the Writings of Bahá'u'lláh,* p. 342.

2. *Gleanings from the Writings of Bahá'u'lláh,* p. 144.

3. *Gleanings from the Writings of Bahá'u'lláh,* p. 268.

4. *The Hidden Words of Bahá'u'lláh* (Persian), no. 40.

5. *The Hidden Words of Bahá'u'lláh* (Persian), no. 21.

6. *Tablets of Bahá'u'lláh,* p. 244.

7. *Gleanings from the Writings of Bahá'u'lláh,* p. 33.

## *Prayers from Bahá'u'lláh*

1. *Prayers and Meditations by Bahá'u'lláh*, p. 4.

2. *Prayers and Meditations by Bahá'u'lláh*, p. 4.

3. *Prayers and Meditations by Bahá'u'lláh*, p. 6.

4. *Prayers and Meditations by Bahá'u'lláh*, p. 76.

5. *Prayers and Meditations by Bahá'u'lláh*, p. 17.

6. *Prayers and Meditations by Bahá'u'lláh*, p. 31.

7. *Prayers and Meditations by Bahá'u'lláh*, pp. 33-34.

8. *Prayers and Meditations by Bahá'u'lláh*, p. 75.

9. *Prayers and Meditations by Bahá'u'lláh*, p. 54.

10. *Prayers and Meditations by Bahá'u'lláh*, pp. 47-48.

11. *Prayers and Meditations by Bahá'u'lláh*, p. 48.

12. *Prayers and Meditations by Bahá'u'lláh*, p. 30.

13. *Prayers and Meditations by Bahá'u'lláh*, pp. 30-31.

14. *Prayers and Meditations by Bahá'u'lláh*, pp. 29-30.

15. *Prayers and Meditations by Bahá'u'lláh*, p. 71.

16. *Prayers and Meditations by Bahá'u'lláh*, p. 53.

17. *Prayers and Meditations by Bahá'u'lláh*, p. 56.

18. *Prayers and Meditations by Bahá'u'lláh*, p. 54.

19. *Prayers and Meditations by Bahá'u'lláh*, pp. 63-64.

20. *Prayers and Meditations by Bahá'u'lláh*, p. 59.

21. *Prayers and Meditations by Bahá'u'lláh*, p. 78.

22. *Prayers and Meditations by Bahá'u'lláh*, pp. 72-73.

23. *Prayers and Meditations by Bahá'u'lláh*, p. 73.

24. *Prayers and Meditations by Bahá'u'lláh*, p. 37.

25. *Prayers and Meditations by Bahá'u'lláh*, pp. 24-25.

26. *Prayers and Meditations by Bahá'u'lláh*, pp. 35-36.

## *Appendix*

1. *Prayers and Meditations by Bahá'u'lláh*, p. 103.

2. *The Hidden Words of Bahá'u'lláh* (Arabic), no. 63

3. *The Book of Certitude*, pp. 256-257.

4. *Tablets of Bahá'u'lláh,* p. 155.

5. *Prayers and Meditations by Bahá'u'lláh*, p. 6.

## *A Website to Help You Cultivate Your Spiritual Potential*

### *www.globalperspective.org*

This Website is designed to serve the followers of all religions and those of no religion. Its message is universal and relevant to all ages, especially young people in search of a meaning and an enduring purpose in life. It can assist you in the following ways:

- Help you choose your everlasting destiny in the light of knowledge and full awareness.

- Strengthen your faith and cultivate your spiritual potential.

- Help you find the means for creating a more pleasant and peaceful world.

- Offer you a global perspective on God's Plan for humankind expressed in the advent of many great religions throughout history, and in this age through the advent of the Bahá'í Faith.

On this Website you will find "Pamphlets" on many topics, which you can download and print for study and distribution.

## *A Few Bahá'í Centers*

*The Bahá'í Faith is established in over 200 countries and territories, and over 20,000 centers. Here are a few:*

Alaska:
13501 Brayton Drive
Anchorage, Alaska 99516
USA

Australia:
Bahá'í Publications
173 Mona Vale Road
Ingleside, NSW 2101
Australia

Canada:
7200 Leslie Street
Thornhill, Ontario
L3T 6L8 Canada

England:
27 Rutland Gate
London SW7 1PD
United Kingdom

Hawaii:
3264 Allan Place
Honolulu, Hawaii 96817
USA

India:
Bahá'í House
5 Canning Road
Post Box 19
New Delhi 110 001
India

New Zealand:
P.O. Box 21-551
Henderson 1231
Auckland
New Zealand

United States:
536 Sheridan Road
Wilmette, IL 60091
USA

## *Unto God Shall We Return*
164 Pages, $6.00

### *Selections from the Bahá'í Scriptures on the Afterlife*

This is the most reliable and comprehensive source of information on the destiny, reality, and immortality of the human soul.

***Unto God Shall We Return*** portrays a most glorious destiny for those who fulfill their lives' purpose during their short stay on this planet. It shows that death is not a voyage to grave, but to God. This book brings comfort to all those who mourn the loss of their loved ones, and instills hope, peace, and joy by unveiling glimpses of the glories that await anyone who fulfills his mission on earth and joins the host of heaven.

We are not permanent residents of this planet, but travelers on a journey to a new and exciting world:

> Say: "O son of man! Sorrow not save that thou art far from Us. Rejoice not save that thou art drawing near and returning unto Us."
>
> Bahá'u'lláh

> Man is the life of the world, and the life of man is the spirit...Rejoice, for the life eternal is awaiting you.
>
> 'Abdu'l-Bahá

## Dear Reader:

We would like to hear from you. Please share with us your thoughts about this book:

**hugh@globalperspective.org**

**Visit Our Website:**
**www.globalperspective.org**

---

## Evidence for the Bahá'í Faith

Please examine pages 141-150 concerning the contents of these three volumes:

*I Shall*
*Come Again*
522 pages, 5″× 8″

**Lord of Lords**
634 pages, 5″× 8″

*King of Kings*
510 pages, 5″× 8″

The three volumes present hundreds of biblical prophecies concerning the Second Advent and show their unmistakable fulfillment in the advent of the Bahá'í Faith. Investigate for yourself and discover how the promise of *"coming like a thief"* was fulfilled by **Bahá'u'lláh** (meaning *"the Glory of God"*) and His martyred Herald, **Bábu'lláh** (meaning *"the Gate of God"*), who appeared in 1844 and proclaimed the dawning of the Day of the Lord.

Be always on the watch.  Christ (Luke 21:36)

I shall come upon you like a thief.  Christ (Rev. 3:3)

## *Publications by*
## *Global Perspective*

### These books are introduced on pages 141-157

| | |
|---|---|
| *Choosing Your Destiny* (hard cover), 375 pages | $ 12.00 |
| *One God, Many Faiths; One Garden, Many Flowers* (hard cover), 290 pages | $ 12.00 |
| *On Wings of Destiny*, 274 pages | $ 4.00 |
| *A Messenger of Joy*, 112 pages | $ 6.00 |
| *Unto God Shall We Return*, 164 pages | $ 6.00 |
| *The Glorious Journey to God*, 258 pages | $ 12.00 |
| *A Glimpse of Paradise* (DVD or video), 104 minutes | $ 18.00 |
| *Come Now, Let Us Reason Together*, 286 pages | $ 6.00 |
| *I Shall Come Again* (hard cover), 522 pages | $ 16.00 |
| *Lord of Lords* (hard cover), 634 pages | $ 16.00 |
| *King of Kings* (hard cover), 510 pages | $ 16.00 |
| *The Glory of the Father* (hard cover), 329 pages | $ 12.00 |
| *Bahá'u'lláh: The One Promised in All Scriptures*, 234 pages | $ 1.99 |
| *Bahá'í Faith: God's Greatest Gift to Humankind*, 162 pages | $ 1.99 |
| *Bahá'í Prayers: The Key that Unlocks the Heart of Heaven*, 230 pages | $ 1.99 |
| *The Greatest News*, 166 pages | $ 1.99 |
| *Prayers from the Báb*, 150 pages | $ 1.99 |
| *God's 19 Great Little Tranquilizers*, 62 pages | $ 1.25 |

Shipping $3:00

### Order multiple copies from the publisher and receive substantial discounts.

**Telephone** or Fax: 989-772-1432
**Website**: www.globalperspective.org
**Email**:  info@globalperspective.org